Barley Child

Miller Williams Poetry Series
EDITED BY PATRICIA SMITH

Barley Child

Poems

Greg Rappleye

The University of Arkansas Press
Fayetteville · 2025

ISBN: 978-1-68226-269-6
eISBN: 978-1-61075-834-5

29 28 27 26 25 5 4 3 2 1

Manufactured in the United States of America

Designed by William Clift

Cover art: *Answering the Horn* by Winslow Homer, 1876. Oil on canvas mounted to pressboard. *Hackley Picture Fund Purchase, Muskegon Museum of Art, Muskegon, Michigan.*

♾ The paper used in this publication meets the minimum requirements of the American National Standard for Permanence of Paper for Printed Library Materials Z39.48-1984.

LIBRARY OF CONGRESS CATALOGING-IN-PUBLICATION DATA
Names: Rappleye, Greg, author.
Title: Barley child : poems / Greg Rappleye.
Description: Fayetteville : The University of Arkansas Press, 2025. | Series: Miller Williams Poetry Series
Identifiers: LCCN 2024041056 (print) | LCCN 2024041057 (ebook) | ISBN 9781682262696 (paperback : alk. paper) | ISBN 9781610758345 (ebook)
Subjects: LCGFT: Poetry.
Classification: LCC PS3568.A6294 B37 2025 (print) | LCC PS3568.A6294 (ebook) | DDC 811/.6—dc23/eng/20240906
LC record available at https://lccn.loc.gov/2024041056
LC ebook record available at https://lccn.loc.gov/2024041057

For the Survivors and Their Children

Are ye of the living or of the dead?

—West Irish response to an
unexpected knock at the door

Contents

II

III

Series Editor's Preface

Whew.

Damn. This America.

This raucous, malfunctioning, precocious, thuggish, absurdly tender, enviable, poisonous, utterly mercurial snitch of a nation. This bumptious, blustering, broken experiment. This circle of arms, haven for guns and greed, this cult of celebrity, this shelter and sanctuary, this bait for demons and demagogues. This place we call—home.

Like it or not, we're surrounded by our country. It hasn't been easy to watch its many wounds rise to the surface for anyone to see.

And maybe it's my imagination (poets are notorious for their imaginations), but I suspect more people are seeking out poetry to help with the increasingly difficult task of entering the day—screeching at Alexa to STFU, flopping out of bed, and cringing at the day's first headline.

The actual truth, assuming anyone can recognize it anymore, has been in very short supply lately. (Catch any segment of a certain cable news network for all the evidence you need.) It's not surprising that more and more neophytes are eyeing poetry's unfamiliar and untrod landscape, wondering what all the fuss has been about, also wondering if there's any semblance of truth they might stumble upon.

Longtime lovers of poetry are also on the prowl, looking for proof that they've always been savvier than everyone else, that "the truth"—in each and every one of its sneaky incarnations—has lurked in stanzas all along. Because poets are still doing what we've been doing all along—serving as unerring and resolute witnesses, calling it like we see it, and lending lyricism and light to the chaos in an attempt to make the hardest of hard truths a little easier to stomach.

Of course, there's that nagging question: *What is truth anyway?* That query has always been the nagging stuff of nightmares and—lucky us—we writers are asked more frequently than anyone else.

I believe that truth in poetry is realizing the strength of our root, as Ukrainian poet Julia Kolchinsky does here in "On the 100th day of war in my birthplace:" from her spellbinding book *Parallax*:

I am still born

in a country named outskirt, a city
named river, on a street named goddess
of the hunt, born in a government-assigned
apartment where our balcony was my preferred
place to sleep while my papa sang
inappropriate songs about alcoholics treating their dogs better
than their women & a neighborhood Baba
would shout up from the courtyard,

He's ruining the child with that language.

Now, I sing my children to sleep
in that same mother tongue [. . .]

Julia, one of this year's Miller Williams runners-up, came to this country as a Jewish refugee in the early 1990s. In her poems, she clutches at a feeling of home that is both unfamiliar and deeply treasured, longs for all that was left behind, struggles to come to terms with the rampant violence devastating a landscape that still, in so many encouraging and heartbreaking ways, belongs to her.

After reading Julia's manuscript, I could only sit with its cogency, reflecting upon its fierce lyric and how an oft-told story—that of the distant daughter of a country now embroiled in war—takes on singular force. These are poems of the unsettled moment, urgent and restless, deftly crafted to illustrate how war becomes part of the migrant's body, how its sole purpose is to change what truth truly is.

In John Allen Taylor's *To Let the Sun*, another of 2025's stellar runners-up, the truth is resolute and resounding. It troubles the poems the way a bomb troubles what dares to surround it.

There is no one who lives this life unbothered. We are all, in some way, wounded. If you are a conscious human of hurtin' age, it's a given that your heart is breaking as you read this. Loved ones die, fortunes are lost and made and lost again, reputations crumble, diseases slash lifelines. Our bodies are pummeled, ignored, taken for granted, invaded. We constantly strive to fold and carve and mold ourselves toward normal.

How?

Poets write our way into the lives we envision. But first we must write into and past the wounding.

That's so much of what John is doing in *To Let the Sun.* He does so without hiding in the squeaky folds of sentiment or resorting to the tired language that latches itself to trauma. In these captivating poems, there are regrets dissected, pain tugged to the surface, love celebrated, secrets searching for voice.

Here. The opening lines of John's heartrending "Golden Pothos":

> I refuse to imagine
> a changed past, another
> childhood. *What if he*
> *never touched you?* she asks
> & I shrug into my cowardice
> *I don't know, I do not know.*
> A pothos hangs over us
> where we sit on the bed.
> The vine doesn't know summer
> rages outside the window,
> doesn't fret about the next
> watering, doesn't remember
> falling from its perch
> on the drive from Boston
> to Detroit when we moved
> last July. It remembers
> the shears, after.

If you ended that passage with a sudden intake of breath, you're not alone. I too was spurred to experience the largeness of moment through the smallness of what the poet allowed me to see. In this poem, as in so many others in *To Let the Sun*, I heard the thick thread of once-suppressed pain woven throughout the now out-loud lines. I heard the wounding, and I was spellbound as John went about his necessary work. But these are not—as we hear all too often—"poems of healing." These memories bellow and screech instead of whisper.

Once I'd made my manuscript selections and learned John's name, I spent hours reading his forays into the minefield, his crafting of truths with their tangled beginnings in the mind of a child, now splendidly wrought in the hands of a poet whose dazzling and devastating poems are his root to the world.

As John declares in "Confession,"

> Only a razor in a steady hand
> could have left this mark.

If you ended that couplet with a sudden intake of breath, you're not alone.

When normal respiration resumes, read this snippet from "Alarm," an offering in Lena Moses-Schmitt's *True Mistakes*—the third of our runners-up (these are in no particular order, by the way).

> This morning, the sound of water rushing underground.
> I don't know what this means, or where the source.
> As if I'm walking on a paved-over river. Fossilized current,
> old patterns of thought. What am I grieving?
> A few blocks away, a truck backs up,
> releasing a slow series of beeps, endless
> ellipses, and I realize it's the same
> alarm that's been going off inside me,
> distant and silent, all year.

What *are* we grieving? The truths we're forced to confront are the thousand answers to that single question. Grieving is a constant. As I'm writing this, the television in the next room blares with news of another child wielding an assault weapon, another school haunted and slapped quiet, another four lives lost. Tomorrow we will reenter the world, warily meet each other's eyes, and nod imperceptibly, acknowledging our ritual of shared terror.

Lena is who we are when we're back in our rooms alone, pummeling the mirror with questions that leave scars. After all, the first truth must be always us—and *True Mistakes* is a lyrical surface for our vulnerabilities, an admission that the human family, for all its boisterous songs and bright colors, is a family of fracture.

The tender but forthright avowals in *True Mistakes* are ones I recognize and have struggled to hear. In these poems, Lena is in frank conversation with her flawed, confounded, and tentative self, and within that revelatory dialogue lurks a truth for every reader.

And now. [FANFARE]

When you happen upon an unforgettable manuscript written by someone you have never met, you instinctively begin to formulate a picture of the poet. You assume educational backdrop, ethnicity, hometown, time spent as a poet, political leanings, creative influences, family life, etc. You can't help it. You're often wrong, sometimes you're right. But you can't help it.

I pictured someone very much like Greg Rappleye, but—and this has nothing at all to do with physical bulk—I didn't picture quite as much of him as there actually is. Not even close.

That said, there's a lot that goes into being Greg Rappleye—winner of the 2000 Brittingham Prize in Poetry, revered teacher at Hope College in Michigan, a frequent presence in the savviest lit journals, and the artist behind the most impressive manuscript in this competition. (Yes, yes, I know—*arguably*. But what the judge says goes.) He's a solid, upright, immensely talented poet who (here comes the part that threw off my conjured portrait of said poet) just happens to write nerve, sonically explosive lines like—

> But above all our American nights, this was legend—
> screams, wingéd ashtrays, shattered bottles,
> a wall splattered with blood that would copper-brown
> as a martyr's relic, holy and untouched,
> into a new millennium, the Philco and its duct-taped
> bunny ears, chucked out the door to smithereens,
> the berserk words tumbling through spittle
> flecked lips and *Looney Tunes* lipstick,
> the syllables of which we knew
> were mortal sins the nuns would drag us off
> to confess were we to chant them, in sing-song
> voices, on the whirl-around at St. Mary's School,
> until Mam was locked in the bathroom
> slashing at air with a straight-edge,
> primed to cut Da's throat, and Da outside the door
> flailing with a spike maul, shattering fat-wood
> to smoker chips, and my sister, age 8,
> came whispering to our rooms.

Uh, wow.

Barley Child goes on and on that way, full to bursting with heat and motion and sound and rampaging narrative, rich with human triumph and frailty, populated with memorable characters whose lives waste no time entering our own. I read the entire manuscript out loud, reveling in the energized unreeling of narrative, the robust characters, but most of all, the unrelenting *song* of it all.

There's no way to read *Barley Child* and not wallow in the midst of all that aural audaciousness, no way not to live within its story, no way to close the book after that last line in that last poem and not believe all of it to be true. True in the way that a poet sees truth—as a resolution for anguish, as acknowledging home, as an unswerving bond between sound and story.

Judging this year's competition was insanely difficult. They've all been. Astounding poems are everywhere, and poets continue unearthing truths when we most need them. Thanks to my stalwart screeners, who passed along the very best, you now hold the best in your hands.

PATRICIA SMITH

Barley Child

Because I Wish to Avoid Extravagant Claims, and Because God Is Patient with the Unborn

Among the nascent embryos, I was a poet
of brass-cut oats, of Dingle cheese, of grilled hake

and muck-tilled potatoes, of soda bread
with salty butter. Then she moaned and I was alive-o,

alive, in the cheap seats of a midnight matinee,
halfway through a pint of *Old Crow*

and a rough cut of John Ford's *The Informer.*
Our story: America staggers through the long count

at Pusan. There are Nixon and Roy Cohn, Cyd Charisse,
Frank and Ava on the friable rocks, and after these,

a New Frontier of moonshots and whirly satellites.
But oh! I am coming, too—your tiny blue *babaí,*

loop-strangling, wheezy, cursed,
cutting loose of Mam's pretty pink womb

and a wee bit drunk, baked for the requisite season.
Call an usher! Summon the charnel cart!

A redpoll snaps to blood in a heavenly pine
and God sighs and says *On with it, then.*

So I fold these scraps in oil cloth,
say a knob's prayer for safe passage,

and slide, so shanty Irish, to a wild indigo sea.

I

. . . And the birds and the bloody stars were all far away, and I was somehow very small and very lost and lonely like a child astray in the snow. And anything that happened to me afterwards, I never felt the same about again.

—Frank O'Connor, "Guests of the Nation" (1931)

Portrait of a Woman between 1948 and 1949

—Hughie Lee-Smith

He boxes his paints, brushes, packs an easel,
cigarettes, and sketch pad, leaves campus,
and rides the 9 bus past Cadillac Assembly
each Tuesday and Thursday, to the vast jumble
of Eloise, Detroit's winsome charity asylum,
where the girl who'll be my Mam
is once again a patient. Let's say this time
it's tuberculosis (it probably was),
but these are the first days of streptomycin;
she is no longer infectious, is close to a real cure.
She is restless, so young, and wants to join
the art class, though it's taught by a Black man;
one who doesn't much like *her*, either.
Still, something about her stays him.
Loneliness, perhaps—look at her eyes—and after
a week he asks, May he paint her
in the light of those fall afternoons?
Somehow, she is graced to say *Yes*. They bond,
painter and model, astonishing the nurses,
and work so well we have this—
auburn hair curling to her shoulders, the ropy,
sea-green necklace she must have borrowed
with its berry-like, opalescent pearls,
her scalloped, almost daring black blouse,
her exposed shoulders, arms fallen at her sides,
a backdrop of darker-than-institutional green,
of blackened red-ochre. He has seen
Modigliani's *A Woman* at the DIA, and here
is a similar palette, consumptive if you insist—
though Mam's has lipstick, her skin is more peach—

and he brings the same sadness to this portrait,
for Mam is in Eloise, that sad place,
and I think, Why not? I loved her, too.
I could give all of this a try.

Night Work

> **Barley child (archaic)**: A child born within six months of marriage. So-called because an average farmer plants barley and reaps it roughly six months later. In a broader sense, suggestive of a barley field as the likely place of an illegitimate child's conception.

He hitched his mule and went to plow the field,
the coulter making a first cut, then iron
splitting the fragrant grass, lifting away the earth,

the mule's jaw lathered a salty foam, braying against
bit and harness, against the soil's loosening grasp,
until the field sang to the blades or seeming-so;

until the grass was fully turned and the field cut
in moon-lit furrows. Then he sowed the field
with barleycorns and rains came and weeks rolled

by and knowing what is sown by night
ought be gathered by night, he honed his scythe
and went back to the field—sling-cutting the grain,

binding the cut stalks, propping them up in tipsy
shocks, until a barley child, slap-patted to a likeness
of a true child, hidden in roots and tendrils,

who had suckled mud and tumbled to a hapless shape,
howled as the scythe cut deep at its thigh
and scuttled away as best a barley child might

oozing blood from a grievous wound. And the man,
raging at the presence of a barley child in his field—
afraid to tell the priest, not wanting the shame of it—

followed the blood by lantern-light
through the groundsel, the dock and blackthorn,
until he lost the trail and turned back, unsure of what

he had seen, but vowing to kill the barley child
some other night—after his crop was stilled
and barreled and aged—come the bone-blood

moons of the coming fall, or surely beneath
some other full-moon rising.

Resonator

—1936 National Resonator Guitar, bottle slide

The man on the pine board steps of the house catty-wise
to yours, home after racking whitewalls all night at Goodyear,

picks at his National guitar; a pill-bottle gliding down the neck,
stalling near the mahogany biscuit that fries above the body's

spun aluminum cone. The free fingers of his right hand
strike across the mumble-low of his voice, an elision;

then the bob of that bottle weeping along the frets, notes
floating over Da's woeful garden, that half acre of dirt

he turned, spade by spade—tomatoes and okra, collard greens,
Natchez peppers, asparagus gone-to-fern, Jonny melons,

passing sweet. Chords drift over lost rudd and shiners, above
the tiny teeth and grinning skulls of dead possums, their entrails

and spines laid deep, *To make rich the earth*, your Da once said.
Was he *ever* so biblical? The slide-man plays on, sweating each note,

as the dead weave and gill through the roots, stirring
the cinnamon-stalked rhubarb and those toxic green leaves

gone almost blue that Da, stumble-drunk with *Jim Beam*,
once dared you to eat, a bitterness you will spit the rest of your life,

those stalks near frenzy under the malignant sun, so achy to push
through the rusty fence.

Checker Cab

> To be sure, marriage was no more attractive an option in America than it had been in Ireland. On both sides of the ocean, many couples were miserable.
> —"Irish America" by Lawrence J. McCaffrey, *The Wilson Quarterly*, Vol. 9, No. 2 (Spring, 1985)

It was a deranged midnight brawl
over rent squandered at the harness track,
or perhaps over a mystery woman who lived
in a second-floor walk-up on Rundle Street.
But above all our American nights, this was legend—
screams, wingéd ashtrays, shattered bottles,
a wall splattered with blood that would copper-brown
as a martyr's relic, holy and untouched,
into a new millennium, the Philco and its duct-taped
bunny ears, chucked out the door to smithereens,
the berserk words tumbling through spittle
flecked lips and *Looney Tunes* lipstick,
the syllables of which we knew
were mortal sins the nuns would drag us off
to confess were we to chant them, in sing-song
voices, on the whirl-around at St. Mary's School,
until Mam was locked in the bathroom
slashing at air with a straight-edge,
primed to cut Da's throat, and Da outside the door
flailing with a spike maul, shattering fat-wood
to smoker chips, and my sister, age 8,
came whispering to our rooms.
She'd crept down the stairs,
descending through a haze of *Lucky Strikes*
and spilt booze, and called for a cab to rescue us.
We tiptoed to the front steps, the youngest weeping,
and even there, the battle-bangs of that fight: the screams,
the assault on that door, echoed across the porch
and through the fizzy, still-sparking tubes of the Philco,

as a vast Checker cab—headlights, top sign, and taillights
glowing—nosed along the curb as if it were
the Cork ferry snuggling to berth, with acres of room
for weepy kids in underpants and half-pajamas.
The cab driver, who took the Host at our church,
sputtered at first, saying No and no to my sister,
but hearing Mam's screams, the crash of glass
and curses, the porch lights snapping up
and down our street, sighed a centuries-old Celtic sigh
then drove without words the six blocks
to our aunt's American foursquare and left us,
knocking up her front door, all for what coins
my sister scrounged, sifting lint from the sugarless sugar jar.
And surely they raged on, or so claim the neighborhood sagas,
with pikes and axes and epic broadswords,
with daggers and cause-lost flags,
wearing the shirt-mail they'd woven from thick skeins
of alcohol and desire, laced through metallic scales
scatter-loose from immense silver carp,
and it did not occur to them when they woke—hungover,
bloodied, bruised, and still coupled for life—
that we were not there. That we were gone.

Age 10, I Escape from the Work Farm and Pursuant to Court Order, Am Recaptured in a Cincinnati Amusement Park

When Big Da finishes me
with the hickory switch,
he says *Your life is too good.*
That's why Mam drinks whiskey.
Frankly, that's why he drinks whiskey, too.
From now on, he says, life is hardtack
and no lard. From now on, life is
channel cats, hot-boxed and nailed
to the rafters of the porch. Henceforth,
the days will be a muddy gruel, boiled
from nettles, scavenged from the rubble-field
where the pig-hut burned—
the flames so hot, the squally hogs
fell over, crackling in their rinds.
Pine tar will teach your tiny trotters
not to wander! Yanked from their nails,
the catfish plump back, rubbed
with clots of buttermilk, as Big Da
sips from a jelly jar and Mam lies
upstairs, massaging her throat,
moaning her trot-line blues, until a crock
of sauerkraut explodes in the cellar,
dangling tendrils of stinky cabbage
from the ducts of the chuffing furnace,
like Spanish moss, strangling the languid oaks
of Evangeline. What indentured child
of God, free-blown of the wreckage
by a vat of fermented kraut, would not seize
such a shiny-dime day? So I, loose-afoot,
patter-step through the moxie plums, so

sweet, singing *Hallelujah! Run for Ohio!*
As if I might *ever* elude Big Da,
his cane-whackers, their scatterguns
and tinfoil badges, their authentic Cajun torches,
his sight-hounds slobbering at my tappers
as I vault across the johnnycakes of river ice,
the judge's name affixed to the writ,
the fine print--pounce-dried and gold-sealed--
impressing the State of Louisiana upon
the creamy white parchment, its whereas-es
and to-wits, the *laissez les bons temps rouler*,
the hereof-fail-not-at-your-perils,
every horrendous legal hokum, until Yours Truly—
cotton-candied, Cracker-Jacked, corn-dogged—
is rat-trapped aboard the Dizzy Teacups
and dragged back behind a three-dollar mule—
hobble chained, belly chained, throat chained,
cuffed; crushed flat beneath Big Da's
punch-drunk, gnarly, geek-show fists.

Angela Sweets, Black Pearls, Columbia Stars

—Sistrurus catenatus

The summer Mam went back to the asylum,
we fell into blackberry fields

and days into dusk, those big enough to drag
a galvanized pail, picked across brambles

of *Angela Sweets*, *Black Pearls*, and *Columbia Stars*.
It was "a nickel-a-pail, full-at-half"—more might bruise

the touchy fruit—but with four of us to pick,
we made our keep those crazy weeks with no Mam.

We browned in the sunlight (our itchy purple hands!)
and the rain would soak our overalls, and wash out

a woeful Tuesday in the windbreak cedars
at the margins of the fields, playing dime-store kazoos

and a muddled game of jacks. I kept a lookout
for snakes. Twice I heard the slightest rattles

of massasaugas, and saw another quicken off
after Julio nudged it with his nail-embedded toad-stick,

but Da was never worried when he pulled
up along the tower road, totaled our nickels,

and, as *weáns* dozed in the way-back of the Nash,
put the car in park under the carny lights

at East Bay Liquors, treating himself to a fresh pack
of *KOOLS* and a brown-paper sack of whatever

kept him sated through those un-pearled
blackberried nights.

Burning Out the Redwings

—Agelrius phoeniceous

The blackberries are a-flesh,
fat with juice, wanting only quick fingers,
but now the redwings wheel and strafe
wherever the migrants pick—
drawing blood, driving children from the field.
So the men block the tower road
spray petrol along the ditch
and (here is the dangerous part) blowtorch
the cattails until, at flash-point,
ethanol claps high along the rush-line
and the already risen birds, panicked,
fall for a dazzling trick
and dive to the cacophonous fire.
Blown aflame, the redwings
corkscrew across the blown-back sky,
arcing like penny rockets, like hissy little meteorites,
trailing sparks as far as the windbreak.
And at dawn, when the children come back
to pick their way to the ashy ditch,
those who dreamed the *scree* of fiery birds
will fill their pails with blackberries.
But having lost a sweet taste,
a simple necessary sweetness,
will no longer eat of the ripened fruit
as they work across the field.

Jack Kennedy Whistle-Stops across Southern Michigan

—October 14, 1960

He glowed in the morning light.
A gasp from the crowd, then wild applause,

the hacks and politicos around him falling away,
his hair, as-if afire—astonishing, an orange-red

I'd never match among my 64 Crayolas.
In the newspaper photo I am there—

against the railroad crossing gate,
holding our grade school's big Irish flag

the other Catholic kids milling about,
wagging their tiny American varieties, and Mam

in awe, nursing a day-breaker pint of *Four Roses*,
her mouth slack and eyes closed,

beside me in a pose of near ecstasy,
of rapture, as if she'd felt the first fine-needled touch

of stigmata, the holy tingles so far bloodless—
just nibbles or mild stings—startling her

palms and feet and side. She is nudging me
toward the train, the slightest weight of her

leaning to my back, edging me to the lectern,
where Jack is at the microphone, pointing

at the Jury-Rowe Furniture Store, the so-azure sky,
into the crisp air, going on about ferritic steels

and good jobs wrenching the big-block Chevys
of tomorrow, and each of us, of every color and creed,

making America more just, better with our special
ethnic dances and crafts, and now I'm reaching

for the step rail, ready to climb aboard the platform,
ready to take Jack's hand in a self-assured

man-boy clasp, to make my pledge
and skip town on his quick black train,

highballing through Chicago, past the hulking barns,
the stock tanks and locust-fogs of Omaha,

to chug at dusk into the vast citrus groves
of the Dream Coast, sipping fresh-squeezed

as the last good waves break high over Malibu
and Dana Point. This was before Semtex cigars

were gifted to Fidel, this was before Marilyn Monroe
in her skin-tight spangled dress, her shoulders thrown back,

exhaled that song at Jack's invite-only birthday bash.
I thought I heard Brian Wilson a-wooh-woohing

Don't worry, baby—though the lyrics hadn't yet
plumped like scones in his Easy-Bake brain—

and I saw our glorious nation entire: gulf-to-bay,
shore-to-shore, from the Sutro Baths

to the pea-green waters of beautiful Nauset,
before this vision fizzled out,

as I was yanked away from the train
and shoved back among the Michigan nobodies—

Jack would live forever, there was a New Frontier,
and soon enough I'd be an astronaut

stepping without care in waffle-soled boots
scouting out a shamrocked crater to plant this flag,

striding nearly weightless
across our not-so-distant moon.

Experts Hope to Blow Out Oil Fire on Tuesday

—*The Marshall Evening Chronicle,*
February 26, 1962

We park in the dead corn (at this point, why not?)
along a county road the name of which I didn't catch
as high-beams washed across its sign.

A quarter mile off, a vast pillar of flame gnaws
the winter sky (leaky valve; a bad-luck rasp of match
to striker). Mam says I must *witness* this night,

ought know the roar of it, must feel the blistering heat,
before Red Adair, creeping behind an asbestos shield,
can poke a jar of nitro at the scorchy wellhead.

Beyond the dead stalks, the whirling lights
of fire trucks stutter against bulldozers,
the pickups, the arcing waters—reddening

the great clouds of steam, washing ochre against
the gravel heap, red across the warped square
of the pipe deck and twisted iron rig,

making it difficult in the other-darkness,
hard against this raging column, in the high-
stink of crude and sulfur, in a sudden flare

of withering heat across boundary snow,
to make many judgments, to know a line of fault.
Why are we here? *To love and serve the Lord,*

Mam says. She skirls the dial across the ionosphere
and snags a border-blast of Mexican radio—all the way
north from Oaxaca—voices we listen to

on late-night drives because they sell "don't worry
powders," "hatchable ducklings by mail,"
and "autographed photos of J. Christ of biblical fame."

Arthur Godfrey

Arthur Godfrey's voice was once the most recognized in America. At one time, he was on radio and television sixteen hours a week with three different top-ten shows and was responsible for 12 percent of CBS's annual revenues.

The floor is checkerboard squares,
dust-rose and dove-gray. A pied cat mewls
under the scuffy dinette. The boy cannot
be older than four, though he can surely reach
the countertop between the Frigidaire
and sink. Mam screws loose the yellow cap
on a shiny bottle and pours a shot glass
of what the boy will one day recall
(if he does not die) as whiskey. She turns,
frantic to pull a burnt slice of soda
bread from the toaster, and suddenly,
the tiny glass-gone-amber summons the boy
in a crow's voice. The caw of whiskey,
a cawed-twice want, thrums in the boy's blood,
calamitous—the clutch of avian feet
on his larynx, on his heart, balanced uneasily.
The boy two-hands the shot glass and takes it
all down, greedy in the spirit, gulping.
He spills not a drop and lowers the glass neat
to the countertop, then falls to the floor, coughs
and coughs—pole-axed, dizzy, lit, but hacks
up no whiskey; his face rosy as the rose-colored
tiles, then ashen as the dove-gray ones.
Mam turns and wonders where her shot has gone
this time, as on the Bakelite radio
the Old Redhead lays down his ukulele,
lights up a *Chesterfield* and half croons,
"How are ya, how are ya?"
into the boy's hot and poundy ears.

Shuffle Puck, 1961

After Sunday mass I'd tap the sponge, touch my head
with holy water, and crawl into the Nash
where Da, settling at the enormous steering wheel,
would ask in his untrue voice, "Dowsie-girl, are ya thirsty?"
Because Mam always was, we'd roll to Gill's Hibernian,
where weekdays you'd hear the blanks at Malleable Iron
being stamped to fender braces for Galaxies and T-Birds.
By then we'd drifted through noon and Pat O'Rourke,
our mail-order private eye, was knee-deep in the malt,
explaining the finer points of blue flashbulbs
and his black-and-gold Studebaker Hawk,
a car that could spin #47 slag from each rear tire
and quick-scoot—lights out—from any motel
parking lot. All I wanted was a game of shuffle puck
on the table Gill salvaged for a hundred-dollar palm-fold
after the grease fire at the Knights of Columbus,
a 22-footer with charred varnish and a hard-rock
maple top that reeked of lake perch and coleslaw.
Gill claimed it was now "flame cured" and wouldn't warp
in dodgy weather. For a kid without quarters there'd be
two pucks left on the table, one red, one blue,
and no sand to float the weights but for that scattered
by the last-calls of Saturday night. I didn't mind; scram-
bling end-to-end, I'd drink *Vernors* on ice with toothpick
maraschinos and play a sort of "knock-off," red against blue
or vice-versa—the slow-mo float of the puck
along maple, the baby *tunk* when red might nudge blue
to gutter. Mam and Da would sink through the *Jamesons*
and peel boiled eggs, sprinkle them with salt, and argue
about those late-payment pinks from Beneficial,
and because I must have cosigned every promissory note
(though all I had to show for this was a cracked yellow radio

on which I listened to static and the Red Wings),
when we got home Da would smack me up the head
and curse a jumble box of curses, then toss me
out the door as if I were a mis-stamped fender brace,
and all those Sundays into dark I'd think on mysteries
and slick pennies down the long black hood of the Nash;
whichever landed closest to the hood's drop to chrome
without going over crowned winner, and loser smacks
his own head twice, with fender-drops tallied
only to break a tie.

I'm Never Told of Family Funerals

—Sitta carolinensis

Not since the wake when I was nine,
when I stole a cushion from Benny's couch
and propped Aunt Rose high in her casket,

sliding a *Pall Mall* between her fingers
and a bourbon tight in her grasp,
nestled among the amber decades of a cut-glass

rosary they'd looped through her veiny hands,
a relic she'd carried home from Lourdes
the summer after the Salk vaccine,

when the greater aunts said Surely now, the Blessed Virgin
would cure Aunt Rose of polio. No matter.
In the afterlife, I knew Aunt Rose would toss

away her brace, her crutches, and two-step
among the American Beauties; that not even Jesus
would begrudge her a party smoke

and splash of whiskey, once he'd seen her dance.
When they came from the rollicked kitchen
to her casket in the parlor, Uncle Jim laughed

as the greater aunts shuddered and crossed themselves.
Father Cusack yanked me by my ear to the front porch
and tumbled me to the rain, to contemplate sin

and my vast effrontery to God.
I hid in the back of the cavernous old Nash
and smoked the last cigarette I'd cadged

from Uncle Jim's coat pocket, coughing and drooling,
praying hard to the Virgin, offering myself up
that I might somehow be saved.

And from that day, the oddest of my dead
have fluttered through my dreams. Sweet nuthatches,
nodding, *wheet-wheeting*, so eager to explain.

That Fall

> CATHLEEN (begins to keen): It's destroyed we are from this day. It's destroyed, surely.
>
> —JOHN MILLINGTON SYNGE, *RIDERS TO THE SEA* (1904)

We knew that salt cod is hideous,
fouled with *nematodes*, its gravy worse,
but had cartoons and were safe enough
for now, watching a frantic mouse drop anvils
on the head of a furious cat. We'd moved
north to Bobby Eagan's, west of Marquette,
his sleek red convertible angled out
along the Superior cliffs, its creamy top
snapped tight against the lake wind, Old Bob
sipping bourbon, eating smoked chubs,
greasy fingers sorting the jumbled wires
of a classified gadget he'd cobbled up
in a fish house near the Soo.
A Western Electric crew followed him around,
burying Bob's secrets across the Keweenaw,
his wires wormed down deep, *To listen*
among the depths, was all Bob would say;
to catch a Kremlin voice, strayed across the Arctic.
I can still hear her along those cliffs, singing
as the big men wrenched and welded and dug,
her blue sweater gathered about her ribs,
raucous terns wheeling, and those saltless waves
heaving cold against the copper-gorged
rocks, her lyrics unknowable—some slurred,
some Irish, though Mam's songs
in those days were already *atonic*,
a word I'd know soon enough,
and sad beyond the other songs of earth.

The Adoration

You walk to the Star-of-the-Sea Church
on Saturday morning, a buttery moon melting
over Polly's and leaves rustling at your feet,
so that, for two hours, you might be sole witness
at the Adoration of the Eucharist—a spotless Host,
a candle-lit monstrance, and the dark of a nave
still with last night's incense; a redolence
in the morning air, where you are not alone after all.
You saw Mrs. O'Neill slip in by the alley door
and hear Mrs. Demay, Chairwoman of the Mary Circle,
fussing below the stained-glass of Christ
calling his sailors to Heaven. You are first altar boy
and must kneel without yawning; stay awake
with aching knees and stiff back until the Ruffing twins
show up to serve mass, by which time Mrs. O'Neill
will have vanished and Mrs. Demay will have said
a last prayer for her son Kevin, already a lance corporal
at Chu Lai, but not before Coach Crowley,
rosary in hand, begins a novena for his wife
Suzanne, who has what the women whisper about
and will be gone next July. Soon enough you'll rise,
remove the vestments of an altar boy, the surplice
and cassock, hang them in a dingy gray locker,
and after a nod from Monsignor Hardy—his cough,
his lonely throat-clearing, booming across the dark—
walk home kicking at maple leaves and, past
the Protestant cemetery with its iron fence
and tall statues of their Civil War dead,
dreaming of Nora Costello, the prettiest girl
in fifth grade, let yourself in by the side door
and pour a bowl of Cheerios, splash it with milk,

and sit out on the back steps for half-an-hour or-so,
watching God gather up the miraculous light
from the stubble field beyond the battering furnaces
of Lefere Drop Forge and press it all across the sky.

Reliquary

Until the water comes sweet
the artesian bubbles a slurried clay—
for three days, an acre of blue marl
swamps the brassy wellhead.
I'm kneeling at the mire's edge
with mollusk shells, with a water-strider
plucked from the creek, with pine needles
and oak leaves and tough little acorns
a-loose from trees atop the hill.
Da's dream is to pipe what good water comes
to an orange-painted shack
he's building; to stir up dark root beer,
to sell cheeseburgers and chili dogs
and greasy chips all summer
to tourists ferrying out to the island.
My dream? To press these shells,
this dead shiner, all sassafras and seed cones,
to the quick blue clay, sure these will dry,
harden to fossils I might varnish, number,
and glue into a cedar box;
to scrawl dog-latin names for each
and amaze the many children I'll have
in thirty years or-so. Who could have known
when the rain came in torrents
my relics would wash away,
that sweet water lasted but twenty years
until a leach of rancid fry grease spoiled it
and that through those cold decades
the madness that drove calamities against the pines,
that gouged and surged across the frozen lakes
and down the Sturgeon R. every damn night
would mold a boy's heart into stone?

St. Brendan and the Foaming Sea (1964)

> When the fish heard Brendan singing, they came up from the bottom and began to swim in a circle round the boat—in such a way that the brothers could not see beyond the fish anywhere, so great was the multitude of the different fishes swimming.
>
> —*The Voyage of Saint Brendan: Journey to the Promised Land*

For the Irish Pavilion at the World's Fair and a lovely savings bond (who would not admire it?) I must color the voyage of Brendan, first-finder of the New World, and so I sketch his brown *curragh* as leaky pudding dish—the wrathful waves, the monkey heads of his dizzy monks, all burnt umber and flesh, just poked above the rim, and Brendan, so tall at mid-saucer, arms raised to chant in Gaelic, to command the schools of Atlantic fish; his monks, nauseous in the oarless shell, the shell, whip-tied with apple bark, bound in ox-hides, lashed tight, tarred black against the tide, a sea scrawled sky-blue; and fish—astir on weedy banks, tails looped-to-mouths as Brendan trills a chorus—gray cods, sea bass, bluefish, and mackerels, a cloud of alewives, those scuttling pinks; a whirling screen of krill—all begin to spin round his tippy muffin cup, raising fish-wakes, foaming, frothy, faster as I bend to task, biting my tongue and bearing down, a child on the cusp of good and evil, knowing what is at stake—Jack Kennedy gunned down, Oswald dead, our Holy Church in perilous flux—my sixty-four Crayolas, an angelic scent of wax—oh, seraphim!—the shad bright then fading, obscure through a distant turn and glitter—purple, red, green and blue, silver and gold—to fire the spins of the tailing fish; their wakes and fishy trails, gluing paper hake and tails of pollack, gluing tiny elvers to foolscap, fish so panicked, they mean to leap free of this page if not for the wheely birds; the shearwaters and noddies, those ravenous auks, if not for a power come wholly upon me to loop them tight, to glue the strays, to cawl them at the gunnels of this pie-tin boat, their captive fins flutter-patting a glitter surface—but for a monstrous octopus, eyes aflame, who suckers a rock, squirts a cloud of midnight-blue and will not whirl away; a lemon sun vast as Brendan's fabled halo, which I last touch orange-red, and America, not far beyond the swells, always meant for a fog-bank in the middle-distance, and there, a sea-light turning in the tall mist and a foghorn resounding as a great trumpet, hailing us grateful to port.

Turnips

> This root, when boiled, has ever been considered as safe a vegetable for the invalid as any in the vocabulary of esculents; and even the fevered invalid, when prohibited all other vegetables, has been allowed to partake of this, not because of its nutrition, but because of the absence of it, not having sufficient to injure the weakest body.
>
> —ASENATH NICHOLSON, *ANNALS OF THE FAMINE IN IRELAND* (1851), CHAPTER VI (2)

So in her Traveller days, when Mam did what the doctor
told her not to and drank whiskey over her blood pills
and her flesh went haw-berry red and purple veins bulged
along her face and shoulders and arms, and tiny vessels
burst in her eyes, turning her a *cosúlacht* of that frightful
Red Hulk of Marvel's *Fate of the Hulks*, a she-beast
whose tricks were howling rage and an urge to catch fire,
she boiled turnips in brine, until the snail-back reeked
of them, and shawling her head, she inhaled turnip-steam
and drank turnip broth, then slowly worked the softened roots
and butter pats to a lukewarm paste and ate what she could
keep down with a tea-and-honey chaser, until the pills
were gone from her and all whiskey gone too and her body
shriveled to a kind of human form and for a time she was small
and pink and no longer screaming and could no longer spark
from tinder-wisp to flame.

In a Dream, My Father Decides to Go Ice Fishing

Da calls collect from Hell. Says, Spud a hole
through the candy-ass ice. Hammer our sign,
blood red, above the shanty door.
He's not here for pickerel. Not come for bluegills,
big as your useless hands. He's trolled this trench
on squalid summer nights, has milted the eggs
and sunk a battered Nash to build a reef;
has nursed these schools from glowworm sprats
and is going deep again—after bull huss and viperfish,
after alligator gar, after hagfish and snakeheads,
all gilling across the silt of our secret spot;
their needle-teeth, banjaxed eyes, and grisly heads,
their hellish Miltonic fins. Whatever we hook
we'll toss, gasping onto lake-ice, scattered out between
the shanty and the sled. So cold they'll be frozen
before they recall open water, as we smoke and shudder
and drink. And which of us, my prodigal, will
stumble out under wolf moon and blistering stars,
tally the hoard, and have a final sip as the other
drifts away? Who'll rise before dawn, stack the sled
with carcasses, and leaving the last to dream alone,
drag our dead back to the morning shore?

The Washpoosh Man

—1967

He'd come tumbling down Randolph Street
crying "Washpoosh! Washpoosh!"
those days he'd slip free and fast-walk
past Mam's sorry rental—his mouth a-grimace,
a wool cap pulled low over his musk-melon head,
galoshes, flannel shirt buttoned at his throat,
and loose tail flying, eyes darting quick
past the reseda and muscat twirls
toward the ice house and herring sheds beyond.
We'd make little screams and swoon behind parked cars
and when his ancient father came trotting down
the hill, shouting "Where's Declan?
Where's he gone?" We'd pop up and point
toward Stoddard Lane, angling away two blocks
north, where the Washpoosh Man might be
at the Rexall scrounging for penny candies,
or worse, at the tavern across the way,
hand flagging at his *dada* mouth, miming for a beer.
If Elaine O'Meara was counting pills at Rexall,
she'd sneak Declan some Bit-O-Honeys
or a few pieces of butterscotch, wrapped
in crinkly yellow cellophane, before walking him
to the door. But if he went for the tavern
there'd be that busted Rock-Ola and surly long-
liners with codfish knives hidden in the cabs
of their battered pickups, ready to torment Declan
in ways Dexedrine and sloe gin might demand,
unless Perfect Ed was wiping the bar that day
in his bow tie, white apron, and starched shirt,
as he'd seen barmen dressed at an oyster house
in Boston. Near the taps he'd lay a baseball bat,

pull Declan a short draft, scrape the foam, and go on
about the Red Sox or the scuttlebutt from Khe Sanh
(our town had Marines there—dug in, thumping mortars),
as Declan stood at the bar, mewling "Washpoosh,"
but quietly, in those few moments after
he'd found refuge; all before his ancient father pushed
through the ding-a-bell door, mumbled a hard oath,
and tugged at Declan's cuff to lead him home.

Shagbark Hickory

—James B. Gannon
1868–1943

"Somewhere on the hill," I'm told,
and in half-an-hour toeing grass, I find his stone—
flat laid, cut plain, but for his name and dates.

I have a photo of him. Have nothing that he owned.
He's dead and not likely to speak, though it hardly matters.

Aside from sea coots, from quahogs nestled in dulse
and tall wicker baskets, aside from wherry-slang names
for sand dabs and croakers, would we even share a language?

The cemetery rolls away, raveling along the field,
a hickory tree rises very near the fence row

and on his grave, within the tree's shady compass,
are two hickory nuts, randomly downed in a quick-storm wind,
tiny nut-kins, still quartered tight in their green rinds—

objects I pocket as useful signs Gee Da might have
meant for me, legacies to be puzzled over,

though I was born ten years after his death,
I sing few elegies, and he couldn't have dreamed
my shoes might ever scuff across his name.

To Recite the Mysteries

He would cast about in his mind for some words that might
console her, and would find only lame and useless ones.
—JAMES JOYCE, "THE DEAD"

Riding my bike home from Polly's with a fresh *Mars Bar*
when two prowl cars hustling without sirens
and an ambulance—white, red crosses—swept
past and, four blocks on, pulled up at the office of Dr. Brennan,
our neighborhood dentist. When I'd pedaled that far,
there were shouts from inside the building and the thump
of body against wood. Someone yelled, "Is the shot ready?"
a curse, then a woman's voice said, "Don't hurt him!"
Soon the cops and white-clothed ambulance men
rolled the dentist out, his eyes like cloudy marbles
thumbed at the gray sky, strapped to a gurney and in a restraint
that made a thistle-heart gasp, "That's a straight-jacket!"
Mrs. Brennan stood in the doorway with one hand against
the frame, and Anne Brennan, in a sky-blue dress,
the smartest kid at St. Mary's School, sat on the steps
and wept; a girl who seldom smiled, but knew the Sorrowful,
Joyful, and Glorious Mysteries and every fruit thereof
and could recite them all whenever called in catechism class.
There were witnesses. O'Toole from the *One Stop*, Mrs. Cullen,
the Gossip Sisters. Of course, the Rumlers showed up,
smirking and fingering their gumball penknives
in the pockets of their corduroy pants.
Decades later, let's say the boy with the *Mars Bar*
wasn't in love with the weepy girl in the sky-blue dress—
though he felt more pity for her than he could explain
and did not want to see her cry. I kept silent
but recall she looked at me as a bird might study
a similarly wingéd bird—familiar, complicit; a look more
than passing. The ambulance pulled away, Anne and her mother
followed in the lead prowl car, and the second cop stared

at us with his hands on his hips, as if to say, "Go home,"
then said exactly that to O'Toole, the others, and me.
I suppose Anne's father spent the night on 2 North,
the local psych ward, and after that, who knows?
Someone said he was taken to a happier place in Illinois,
where they'd lived before coming to our blown-gasket town,
an hour west of the giant tire along I-94 that shouts
This is Detroit to anyone still listening. No matter.
A sign went up in the smudge of his window,
Anne never came back to catechism, and the office
was sold for a hair salon. Can you name the happy places
left in Illinois? They don't even make *Mars Bars*
anymore, though there are times an ambulance passes
(lights, siren wailing) I can taste the nougat,
the toasted almonds, the caramel, and chocolate.
Wherever Anne Brennan is, she may recite
stray phrases from the mysteries she once had by heart—
"I cannot be consoled . . . ," or "How lonely it is,
that once crowded city." Perhaps she wakes
during slow-rain nights and gathers the raveled threads
of her story—radio traffic and sirens, the first cop
nudging a punked *Camel* out the prowl car window;
Evergreen to Bridge Street and crossing busy Cortland,
the burnt-clay bricks of the hospital walls.
Who was the breathless buzz-headed boy
straddling a one-speed with panic in his eyes, socks
fallen round his ankles, and a *Mars Bar* held out—absurdly,
almost as an offering? What did he want then
and does he wonder where she is now?
How her life might have changed had he shared
the candy bar, maybe touched her cheek in pity;
useless efforts, he'd always known, to make
and keep her safe.

Greetings

> He was close to home and far away,
> always loving it, always hating it.
> —James Matthews, *Voices: A Life of Frank O'Connor* (1987)

Your dead begin to whisper
among themselves. *He is coming,*

one says and brooms the cobwebs
from the sash. *He'll take a glass*

of Irish in the afternoon, says another
and finds a bottle in the pantry,

turns the label face-out and sponges away
the dust. Your dead are forgiven

by God, they claim
and will no longer stand to account

for how you feigned sleep
through the chokecherry afternoons,

for the welts across your back
you would not explain to the nuns.

Even you, walking this last walk,
might forgive them. Tomorrow, perhaps,

further along this path, you will
lay down the weight you've carried

for years. Everything you truly own,
jammed in your star-sewn valise, grows

heavy, so tiresome to wonder at,
to show-and-tell, without stopping

along a curb to haggle a short-sale,
to leave packets unclaimed

on doorsteps and windowsills,
to lay out pearly marbles, feathers,

nickel candies, your old set of jacks,
all gathered in marvelous foils, one small gift

for each, among the bundles of the poor.
You cannot know how hungry you are.

That a shoulder roast—braised, simmered
that long afternoon in red wine,

with April leeks, carrots, potatoes,
and garlic cloves, with basil and oregano—

waits for you. That the table is laid
with a hodgepodge of silverware

and the old blue china.
That there are soda bread and marmalade

on the sideboard and cool water for your great thirst.
That a fire has taken in the hearth,

is coming to blaze as your dead rise from their chairs,
smooth their aprons, button their cuffs,

and check the clock ticking upon
the dark mantle, its main-spring fused tight

to a blasting cap, ready at last
to welcome you home.

II

My heart feels not so much in my chest as in my hands. I am carrying it along swiftly, as though I have become the messenger for what is going on inside me.

—Claire Keegan, *Foster* (2010)

Beneath the Clock Tower, Main Gate

—Anguilla rostrata
Pepperell Cotton Mill,
Biddeford, Maine

Through the shattered windows,
the cotton bays echo, dark as tubercular lungs.
Here, the looms were chanted to bid;

trolleyed in shimmering rows across the dock
and winched high, Free-on-Board, for Bangkok
and Taipei. Now not sure they are dead,

their work forever gone, my uncles, aunts,
cousins, grandfather—all look up,
check their vacant wrists against the clock,

and report through the slide-away door.
Who can I name among these photographs?
Little Andre, the Coté boys, and Willie,

I'm sure of. Is that Norah Burke? It could be.
Night-knocker, help me name the others.
Who among these split wide

the cotton bales, who loaded the hopper?
Whose barefoot child wept quietly and retied
the broken threads? Who oiled, who swept,

and who pulled down the battens,
ran calloused fingers along each worn edge,
jig-cut the same old shapes, then planed

through dawn and reset the looms?
Who bull-racked the finished cloth? Who cut?
Who packed and loaded and shipped?

And who can say where each one stood
their ten-hour days, calves and soles aching,
shifting from one foot to the other,

and the names of the mill bosses they once cursed,
their grievances and what was left unsaid?
Should I not stand at the gate and hand out lyrics

to Wobbly songs as, single and double file,
my dead report for work—old Seamus,
clutching a lunch pail to his chest,

those Killarney Girls, hair braided back,
smiling and holding hands—announce them in song
as I check off their names, insert their cards,

and clock them in, perhaps brighten
Benny's cup with a splash of *Early Times*?
If banished from this gate, at what great door,

along which wrought-iron fence—
at dawn or at dusk—should I wait?
The river comes all hurly-tide, with a tumble

of seabirds—frantic in the sky; feeding.
If the mill race is frozen, must I walk across?
If not where the dead gather,

from which shore of the estuary, only now
beginning to swirl with these translucent glass eels,
must I stand away and sing?

The Marsh Harrier

—Circus aeruginosus
Nora Gannon (1881)

I need not name them—the poet who lured
me to the granary near Belmullet and took me
against the barley sacks. Nor the louche painter
who sought my portrait and had much more

in the startling sea-light at Céide Fields,
and the several others among that rakish lot,
until, by the Eve of St. Foillan's Day,
no one knew who might be the Da, though

swayed by my condition, all thought it best
to have the muffin out. So a plate was passed
among the six, a collection made of farthings
and shillings and half crowns—fair-as-fair,

from each according to his abilities, etc.,
along with a pity's pence from my cousin,
then a four-day reach from Mizen Head
in Alf Bannion's herring sloop,

not slowing to lower nets in days it took
for passage to the docks at Plévenon
in Brittany, one of Seven Celtic Nations,
so told. Left among the midwives of that place,

both crone and near-physician, I was given teas
of artemisia and pennyroyal and when, after two days
the plum had not sprung its grip, I was ragged
with a fist of ether, and what ought be done, was.

A week I rested; staring across the thorny gorse,
then wandered the cliffs at Cap Fréhel,
near the ancient abandoned light tower, with the gray
Atlantic keening, slap-dashing the rocks below.

On the agreed day, I returned to the docks
to find Alf's sloop, packed with German rifles,
black-powder cartridges, and a dozen revolvers,
all swamped about with nets and silver herring.

Was it best I made the trip? The men got
what they'd come for and, anyway, the *weán*
was a girl-child, and would've been of small use
in the dreamed-of rising. As memento, I've kept

only this short-list of Breton birds—guillemots,
red-billed choughs, stonechats, and a marsh harrier
among them, the last of which I'd watched
stunting above a boggy field, diving at a red fox

that trotted through the willow-strife
and sandy hummocks, patiently searching out
the marsh harrier's earth-nested young.

My Grandfather's Herringbone Cap

> Among the working classes, the fishermen and millworkers, the Maine [Prohibition] Law is but gauzily enforced, and it is common to see hopelessly besotted Irishmen stumbling through the Five Points, their minds consigned by alcohol to the deepest states of vice and immorality.
>
> —Report of the Citizens' Select Committee, Biddeford, Maine (1905), p. 4

Fish-stained, sloe-ginned, spotted by
bean soup, cocked atop his fuddled head,
the cap's chevron weave looks as if
he's mauled through a case of split
herring and dealt the filets about his skull
in circled rays, skeleton-upon-skeleton,
each tail pinioned beneath the cap's
top button, and brislings fanned away,
the bones orbiting and slowly gathering
depth, layer upon layer of tweedy
articulated bones—all shoaled across
his bald spot and schooled within his skull,
still and then startled, their pickled kin—
whiskey-lit shad darting lobe-to-lobe,
from synapse to synapse. His body lurches
to a pause, then wanders as to sea—
stumbling, left arm cast away for balance,
the brim of his herringbone cap,
as if the relentless jaw of a mackerel
slashing through a bait-cloud, trailing ribs
and spines from gill rakes, the air gone
entirely wrong and nausea churning his gut.
His cap spins to street-cobbles,
the shiny satin lining—its maker's mark
lettered in gold filigree—goes sky-up.

Comes then a faint clang of sea-bells,
heard by every drowned man,
it is said, sinking below two fathoms,
and the crowder bar of this net—
pushy, so pushy in its work.

Grievous Angel

—Francis Burke Gannon, Age 7,
diphtheria, July 19, 1910

Gran laid a wet cloth above his brow, a bowl
of soup cooling at the bed rail, then left for the mill
and that night his soup untouched, membranous
with chicken fat, little Frankie spiking hot
and rattling a cough that scoured the lungs
of those who stood helpless at his bed and hugged
their ribs in panic and a growth like tree lichen
all slopped across the back of his throat.
Then Gran, weeping *He's got the bull neck,*
pulled Bridget's reluctant little fingers to her brother's body,
making Bridget seek the hot swollen lumps
of his neck glands; making her roll them with two fingers
saying *Now they're the size of cats-eye shooters,*
Now they're hard as Brussels sprouts,
and Gee Da home at last, gin-drunk on his quaky knees
and kissing the knuckle of his gnarled thumb,
pleading with Christ to save his fine boy,
telling Willie, *Fetch the younger priest, dammit!*
And his boy in candlelight, one second raspy
then still; and an angel (from which high corner?)
so deliberate, unrushed, astride the boy's waxy face
like a mantis, drew Frankie's soul from his wee mouth
and clutching it as if a shed skin—limp, diaphanous,
mucous-stained—hopped to the open dormer and free
to the sweltering night and rose above the mill's
clock tower, over the belled spire of the church,
until the angel, finding its necessary air, quickened
in two wingbeats and vanished among the hothouse stars,
far beyond the Wood Island Light.

Cotton House Fire

October 29–30, 1915

True, how could they see anything but the shadows
if they were never allowed to move their heads?
—Plato, Allegory of the Cave

I did not torch the Cotton House
at Pepperell Mill and you cannae prove
I was there after 9 pm, drinking whiskey
from a flask atop the Pascagoula bales
we carted from the dock last week.
Let's say someone *did* have an oil lamp
and was rolling a smoke, with scraps
from a tobacco pouch and the French
wrappers Eddie brought back, Saturday last,
from Portland. Anyone could have bought
those. I say this in speculation and wonder,
as I know not a *bona fide* fact, have heard
but few nasty rumors, and anyway, did not
drop a lit cigarette, nor splatter lamp-oil
down among the bales. There's *nada* proof
I was sparking the magic-flashers
Eddie may have also picked up (so cheap!)
at Culp's Magic City, snapping the papers,
flitting them to air; to illumine, to light
up the Cotton House all sorcerer-like,
casting black shadows, phantasms, great
dark shapes, vastly horrific against the rafters
and brick walls, like a magic lantern show
exactly, like something from Plato's *Allegory*,
a book I did not read—it cannae be proven
I *can* read—the nitrocellulose
crackling, exploding, incandescent,
burning with a brilliant flash, leaving no

ash, no crispy paper residue, tricks I'd meant
solely for the amazement of tenement kids,
for a few rowdy neighbors on Halloween.
When I left the Cotton House there were
no flames at all, no smoke but what curled
from a puffed-out match, from my last roll-up,
which I surely recall grinding to the pine floor,
toeing the butt flat, and no, not dropping it,
ash-orange, down through the cracks
between and among the oily bales, the interior
of the Cotton House otherwise dark as Pascagoula
at midnight, the bolt of the great door sliding back,
latching with a raspy thunk, no reason for
any reasonable man to think, to hope,
that deliria might spark tinder,
that it would come to flame,
that the cotton; that bricks and timbers
would burn all night and collapse in smoking
heaps of brick and ash and glass, of workers'
dreams and scorched soggy bales.

The State of Maine

—The Great Influenza Pandemic,
September–December 1918

The Irish girls board the train at Biddeford,
bound for Camp Devens, with a suitcase between
them and two jars of blackcurrant jam.
Their soldiers, who look a slight off-kilter,
swear they'll carry these treats
all the way to the Somme. The girls smile
to think blackcurrant jam might be wanted
in the squalor of those dank
trenches; to sweeten the soda dodgers
and bum coffee, to help the boys remember
or even dream of them. After a few venial
sins, after a night of giggles in the visitors' dorm,
the girls head back on *The State of Maine*,
iron wheels clacking merrily along the iron rails,
leaving the coach window slightly ajar
because it's a bright September day and fresh air
is best for sniffles and scratchy throats,
not knowing that soon their doughboys
will be frothy-lungs dead; that some fever-days
later, *they* will be dying too, but not before
wheezing death through the Pepperell Mill—
at bale-cutters and spinners and weavers
and carders—and forty years on, the Doyle brothers
will be smoking *Raleighs* at a wake in Saco,
telling a wide-eyed boy how they scrambled
over coffins piled outside the undertaker's
livery, playing blind man's buff, and at dusk
hid among the stones of St. Mary's Cemetery,
watching the Czech gravediggers dump

mottled corpses from those pitch pine coffins
into six or eight autumnal graves,
then stack the coffins onto a hay wagon, shawl them
with a canvas tarp, and roll the empties back
behind the mortuary gate.

Annie Kelly, 25

The Central Maine Sanitarium,
Atwood Mountain, Maine (June 17, 1922)

After Maggie died and he remarried,
I stayed on at Jim Gannon's.

I had nowhere else and each of them so needful
of what I made from the mill.

It was alright for awhile, until McPhee
from the weave room caught me hacking up

a wad of linty snot and saw the wicked
cloud of blood smeared across my cuff.

He called the mill doctor, who pressed
a stethoscope to my back. "You've got TB,

Annie. You're out of work for good."
Jim's Canuck bride cursed me in French

and I smiled behind my breath-mask,
the day the health nurse took my elbow

and helped me board the train.
As tiny spite, I wore Maggie's straw boater,

trimmed with a sprig of snowberries,
pinned against the black band.

To bid us eat ("Eat, Annie! Eat!")
the china plates are lovely—

a creamy white with crimson stripes
milling the edge, a top mark

with recumbent moose and pine, framed
at right by a sailor; left, by a reaper

leaning to his scythe. All of this
topped by the North Star, underlain

with the word "Dirigo," our state's motto,
meaning "I lead" in the language of the Church.

I stare at the plates but feign no interest
in dumplings and stewed lamb. Mrs. Cleary,

who sleeps beside me on the porch, cackles
and says, "Made your bed, girlie, best lie in it."

Though coughing bloody phlegm to a tin bowl,
untangling my sheets each morning I am

able, I cannot believe so little is true.
I am beyond desire, save to go down

from this sleeping porch some breathless night
when the lantern-bugs are lit, to strip away

my sweat-stained gown and, holding my arms
across my untouchable breasts, to fall on

to God down the side of this hill.
I have misled no one—anytime, anywhere.

No one will follow.

Winter Flounder

—Pleuronectes americanus
Biddeford Pool, February 11, 1924

Ungloved to rig. Ten feet of leader, swivel,
dropper line to a pyramid sinker, hook
muscled through a chunk of cut squid—
awkward the toss-out as a tide begins to run.
Let the milky bait drift. When the squid
grows tattered, give tatters to the sea.
Blackberries plucked from bramble
cane, mashed, juiced, razzled in brandy,
and pressed through cheesecloth,
cool in a Ball jar, as scallop boats
chortle through the long afternoon.
The wind grows colder. The sun thumbs
nickels at your eyes. Lower your cap
and turn aside. You want a flounder—
pat-a-cake flat and goggle-eyes up,
its sidelong mouth, its dumbfounded look
if caught, inexplicable as your rent-book,
with its crabbed juggles and subtotals.
Your line is far long. Could it be your bait
has wandered away on shamble-toes
where the river twists across the estuary?
A mess of sculpins, unwanted, lie gasping
at your feet, while the sea stars, purple
as the lung-starved bodies of the drowned,
clamp fast to the weedy rocks. No scallop boats
now. You flop back, fan a flatted angel
to the cold sand, rise, and reel again.

Jim Gannon, with Dog and Model A, January 12, 1928

He stands in the Biddeford cold,
enough snow to say, Yes, this is winter,
and because we have a name and date
penciled faintly on the back, we can
be sure the glowering little man
is Gee Da, and here almost sixty years old.
He looks older than this, of course;
looks tired, nerve-shot, angry
with whomever is taking this photo-
graph along the lap-board rise
of a shabby mill-owned tenement.
Could the photo have been snapped
by Armand Coté, Jim's Quebec
in-law, who had a Kodak Brownie,
sported a mothy beret, and worked
as lead-man over at Diamond Match?
Perhaps, though it's hard to know—
the photographer is nowhere named
and there is not a shadow of a body
washing forward, leaning to a lens,
to a focal point, shadow-gray across
the snowy drive. Jim stands in a wrinkled
shirt, a dark tie, half-Windsored
under an ill-fitting vest, his best trousers
clowning out, a paperboy's cap that hides,
no doubt, a bald spot, Sunday shoes,
no jacket, and no gloves. We also see two
skinny rear tires and the dark, down-curved
rumble-seat lid and canvas top
of a Model A Ford Roadster.
This car cannot be Jim Gannon's.
Too broken now to hustle the big looms,

he's only a ride-along teamster,
an overage delivery boy for the mill,
and could not afford a junky old car,
let alone a new Ford Roadster.
Nor would he buy kibble for a dog,
not one as hapless as this—
a mix of runty Boston terrier
and shad-house mutt. It's a mystery
why Jim holds the dog's leash so
oddly—loop-handle in his left hand,
and the leash, stringing across his vest
to his right, where the cord is held
with only the index finger and thumb
and then down to the sorry little dog—
an affectation, almost twee,
as a desert saint might be depicted
in some Italian painting
from the early Renaissance
holding a sprig of thyme or a tiny
bird's egg for all to see, by which
the viewer is to understand faith,
or the depth of God's love for a lonely
saint, surviving upon the merest trickle
of a nearby spring, upon bread-crusts
dropped miraculously by wheeling
desert birds. But here, we learn
only that the churlish man does not
like this dog. That the dog, tugging
against her leash, pulling sideways
to the scraggly wintered hedge, will yap
and yap, will distend her tongue
up and down against the choke of collar
and lead, and is unwilling to pose,
to still herself within the viewfinder,
because she does not much like the man
who is holding her back, either, a man

so eager to be in his stuff-less chair,
out of this cold, away from the yappy dog
he hates and the car he can never afford,
that he will not smile and welcome us
into the frame. *No,* he says, *Hurry up,*
now, save the pity. Get an eyeful,
ya bastards, and turn the page.

Among the 796 Dead Children at Bon Secours Mother and Baby Home, Tuam, County Galway

Michael Gannon, 18 January 1928,
age 6½ months, general tuberculosis

The wren, calling at dawn from a thick of cedars,
is counted as lost, once she ceases to sing.

Soda-white the winter field, a father unnamed,
and the child gasping a blood-wet song.

Ninety years on, perhaps it's best we let him go—
a sign of the cross, a nod to the near forgotten,

and leave him brooding on his shelf
among the silent Irish dead.

Dowsie Gannon, Age 2, in Cleveland

—April 7, 1930

After he left the doctor's office, Gee Da stopped by church to consult *Butler's Lives of the Saints* and found there was no saint for a bad pancreas. So they sell all but what folds in cardboard suitcases (Dowsie keeps a rag doll) and are chipping fares halfway across America to watch his earthly descent in far-off Jackson, Michigan, where Gran has a sister.

Three times—coming and going, coming again, they have sidetracked and stopped dead for passage of *The 20th Century*, in a rumble of coal and iron and smoke, its singular call, not a whistle, but an echoing horn, a long brassy howl, with red carpets rolled and loop-tied, waiting at both ends of its speedy Chicago runs; Gran saying in her best English, each time more sadly, There goes *The 20th Century.*

This latest train was all-aboard in a Buffalo hailstorm and stops at every junky town that dots the Erie coast, dropping off milk cans and grimy chemical tanks, hooking up an old slumber coach for a short tug to Ashtabula. These stops, the sidetracks, lull the child to sleep. Then, cranky, she startles awake when the throaty Mohawk engine bump-couples or cuts free a short-stack of cars.

It's 4 am. The brake lines hiss-away steam. They are entering Cleveland, Ohio; side-tracking to its station, pulling ever more slowly past Rockefeller's oil works, past the fiery Bessemer rolling mills and the Irish Flats, past the Haymarket and the jolly all-night neon of Sing Long Low Chop Suey.

An hour until the train pulls away. Gee Da eases back on a station bench and drinks deeply of laudanum, as Gran carries Dowsie deep into the big hall, where Dowsie stares at the sun-flowered ceiling—a painted sky, aglow, arcing blue behind the flowers; the wide, black-eyed flowers, like so many bumble-dee bees, like so many be-fuzzled eyes, watching her, *divining*, a word she does not know. Do the *scitsifréine* voices, her Gaelic *pookas*, already mutter?

Dowsie whimpers, she slides to the marble floor and howls, kicks with her sturdy legs and, diaper-less, wets the floor and her cotton smock—drawing looks from passers-by—a Red Cap, a wimpled nun, two sailors on leave from Chicago. *Petite merde!* Gran cries in her native Quebecois, loud enough for the nun to cross herself and blush, to recall her vows as Bride of Christ, as Gran struggles Dowsie up from her puddle.

She carries the howling child, its tiny hands rowing the circumference of teacups, back to nodding Gee Da, pulls the laudanum from his breast pocket, and forces three good drops, maybe more of this tincture of opium and grain alcohol, down Dowsie's throat—who can safely say how much she gave her, more than ninety years on?

It is hot, Dowsie thinks, eyes wide and startled into silence—then to a squall of baby coughs, until she forgets to cough and whatever burns within her body, as, with an iron shrug, *The 20th Century* rumbles by again, its great brass horn howling through the pithy sumac that grows, unchecked, where the fabled train makes such quick work crossing the Cuyahoga River.

Last Letter from Great-Aunt Nora Gannon, Resident at St. Margaret's House of Industry (Infirmity Ward), Dublin, to Her American Nephew, Concerning the Spanish Civil War, John Dos Passos, Etc.

—12 August 1937

If a Fiat Arrow barreled through
the scumbled Dublin sky and scatter-sprayed
incendiaries across the sorry shutters
of this refuse heap, I'd God-bless Mussolini
and step off into the propeller.
But everything's cream and carrot-tops
in your U.S. of America. Rest easy,
nephew, as your dear cousin, Big Bill Gannon,
fights on against the Fascists—last month
marching the Connolly Column through Madrid.
Someone must rise for soda bread and roses,
though I'm sure you gave as good as got
with the shawlies of Biddeford, Maine.

Big Bill writes that he met Dos Passos—
"Dos" to those who know. They tapped a cask
of sherry—cozy is as cozy does—
in a command post near Brunete.
Big Bill is legend for plugging the traitor
Kevin O'Higgins along the Boostertown Road—
Bang! Bang! Bang! Not an ounce of lead
whizzed past the bastard's head!
Well, Dos begged to be posing a photo
with Big Bill, who's a genuine Gaelic hero—
amnestied by de Valera himself—
someone to do a family proud.

The Westie Merrow's great curse
wasn't drink, but cadaverous-long life.
With the grippe again, high athwart my windpipe,
I surely wheeze the last pearly chords
of my concertina. *Squee!*
So I've enclosed a birdwatcher's guide
and my life-list of birds—200-so of Irish-types
and 18 of France, with species totals—
the Frenchies journaled during a hasty trip
to Brittany, taken after your Da skittered
off to Maine and the overgenerous bosom
of your lamentable mother, may the Blessed Magdalene
redeem her bog-slopped soul.

Last to list?
A frazzled bittern, strayed a looney's course
from the Azores, espied slurping eels on the Liffey flats
as the boil-cheeked postulant rolled me out
along our daily stroll, so-called. Silly thing,
she'd snap her vows like sugar peas
and elope with the coal boy, could he hazard
a sober look at her.

A Wild Goose such as yourself
might wire the fare for steerage
and I'd sail for Boston by fall. Once there,
should I hack my death of whooper's cough
amid a ferocious Yankee gale,
spin me in my grave so I look across the waves
toward the cockled shores of West Sligo,
where the wet nurse of W. B. Yeats
hectored me to speak a civil tongue, and where
your precocious cousin Billy, bare a lad of eight, topsied the cart
of the fruit monger, sending cantaloupes
careening 'round the soot-blackened stones
of the market lane, so peckered was he
by the price of Yorkshire plums.

Helldivers

—Curtiss SB2C Helldivers;
downriver Detroit, July 1943

The girl who'll be my Mam is alone,
free of the asylum on a weekend pass,

sprawled on the steps of Maggie's faded two-story,
listening as Helldivers from Grosse Ile

strafe Plum Island, sortie after sortie,
each scored by an ensign aboard a gray tug

buoyed off the mid-line, because "practice makes perfect,"
and our best will be needed at Truk and Iwo Jima.

Not supposed to drink (Amobarbital, too young),
she's on her fourth beer from Waddy's extra ice-

box and is eating blind robins on dark rye—
over-salted herring filets; stinky, the worst snack ever.

She knows that Paul Witkowski, who's slumped
in a wheelchair on the porch of a bungalow

kittied across St. John Street, who lost both legs
and much of his face to phosphor and bunker oil

aboard the *Oklahoma*, will persuade himself
the Helldivers are Japanese Zeros

and begin to scream, sure that he's back
at Pearl; four hours a day, seven days every week

he wails, unless the Helldivers—thumping live ammo
to the Plum Island mud before pulling up

and circling back, their high-horse engines
roaring all the way down Eureka Road—

don't score well enough and need more practice,
sometimes flying deep into the buzzy, mosquitoed dusk,

Paul Witkowski and Mam echoing those perfect
machines wail for wail, scream for scream.

Ventrilo

Throw your voice!
Amaze your friends!
—1950S COMIC BOOK ADVERTISEMENT

Troglodytes troglodytes

Bought in a Saco junk shop and recalled from *Captain Marvel*, it's a tin loop, like a shattered whelk—beveled by waves so as not to cut—by which I once believed a voice might be tossed at all bodies, living and dead. Sugared in rum, against my wintered lips, it throws no voice; merely renders a flutter, a trill, a whirred falsetto song. Listen. St. Stephen's Feast. The Wren Parade. A scatter of snow across herringboned bricks. The wren-boys wander about in straw hats and reedy suits. The captain shouts, a din rises. A canvas horse, rushes tacked along its canvas flank, is made to gallop by a boy's pumping arms, giving chase, or seeming-so, as the wren-boys, their captain, the cacophonous tangles of snare drums and penny whistles, of trombones and bodhráns, begin to unspool; from a jumbled knot to a ragged marching column. At its lead, besieged by revelers—a felt wren, so-sung King-of-all-Birds, is hung from a stripling ash, dead to all, his high-stick ribboned in Gaelic green, in orange, the wren's body dangled in mistletoe, in blood-berried holly, rising above a flag of Mayo, the flags of Connacht, eight flags of a golden harp rampant in a field of green; so many flags of the left-behind places. We sang from memories and lyrics scattered among us—*I have a little box under my arm / a tuppence or penny will do it no harm*—the wren-boys, their feigned surliness, drowning out the beggared words and lost with them, my best try at a wren's true voice, tossing a rush-and-tumble song where I alone chose to throw it—across rye grass, curling through calla and knapweed, warbled across a swale on Oak Street, echoed against the three-story tenement where Gee Da ate fried pogies and coughed a lint-snot cough; tracking his rent in a green notebook, each entry an epitaph, made in a spidery blue script. And no one heard the true song. What is a true song, warbled at sow thistle, whispered from trailing arbutus, from woe-vine, when a ragged parade is loudly passing? We sang without thought, not yet amazed, missing a little point (there may have been others), of how the wren—its throaty squeals, its assault of cuffy scolds—saved Stephen from the Norse, luring them far from a wounded saint and across a darkling bog, until the exhausted bird fell and was killed for its kindness, pummeled, and hung above a great fire—broken-wingéd, blooded, trussed, and bound—the King-of-all-Birds, set aflame; dangled from the Tree-of-Heaven. *Will you not toss a penny*, we sang, *to buy this king a grave?*

III

. . . and I believe the living haunt the dead.

—Karl O'Hanlon, "In the Non-Catholic Cemetery, Rome"

Shotgun Death, with Dodge and Northern Catalpa

—March 26, 1951

How long have they idled, motor throttled
down, off the two-track, at rest on snow-crust
in his '47 Dodge, its chrome bumper
and yellow fog lamps facing the catalpa tree,
the heater madly whirring against
a night gone entirely cold?
The man at the wheel is her first husband,
the woman who will soon enough
be my Mam is seated beside his body,
hand lifting to her lipsticked mouth,
the air of the Dodge so lit, fully blown
of gun-powder, of sloe gin and buckshot,
a waxy shell ejected, clattering
against the right-side dash.
She has bruised an ear drum, she claims,
from the blast of that 12 gauge, hammered
flat at close range. This, the shock,
her bedlamic shriek, will muddle her
thoughts, make it hard to hear the coroner,
to understand the parish priest,
to weep sincerely, some whisper, until
his baffled parents order a marker
from the VFW and drive back to Terre Haute.
How did the pump-action shotgun,
cut to riot-length, its butt at-rest
in the rear foot-well, its coal-blue barrel
angled at the driver's side of the bench seat—
go off? Who clicked three shells into the magazine,
who racked the pump, and was the safety on?
The detectives who rumble out, sirens
wailing, from the far-off county seat,

who swaddle her in wool blankets,
who smoke *Luckies* and toe them deftly
into the snow, who light up her footprints
with blue flashbulbs and prowl-car spots—
they want only sensible geometry
and a few hard facts, but she cannot say
why her husband placed the shotgun like-so,
why they idled, motor lowing, so long into the dark,
why his cob-yellow brains and bits
of seat-fluff stipple her tight pink sweater
and the jaggy blown-out windshield, or why,
high above them, the wintered seed pods
of the catalpa tree—longish, thin,
but for where the adamantine seeds
swell the pods' tobacco-brown casings—
are splattered with the song-less tongue
and silent lips of that long-rumored,
half-hearted man.

At Mercywood, Theodore Roethke Instructs My Mother in the Care and Feeding of Peonies

St. Dymphna: Irish, seventh-century martyr. Patroness of those afflicted with mental and nervous disorders.

In the asylum greenhouse, the moon all
afflux, up through the crazed glass—
with spades, with hoes and a red barrow,
we'll scratch among the dormant ones
and untangle their roots, cutting tendrils,
sorting, culling spoiled eyes from good,
and lay the saved in wire baskets,
hiding them beneath the pine bench.
We'll settle the roots in terra-cotta pots
with loam and compost, wormy, fragrant,
and well drained, and tend to the easiest,
quick to spread, needing only sunlight
and garden lime, peonies with lovely heads,
shaggy and pink, white, lavender, and red,
hardy against the bitter cold. Winter must
pass before these will bloom. And you,
child, *prima donna* of the dayroom?
Ought smile in the ice baths—the ivory tubs
like lifeboats, their tall prows lifted, plowing on
through gray-tiled seas. Near the iron gates,
should pause as the bells chime noon
and mumble your beads. Ought weep for
the hair-raised, the electric, as they are rolled
back to their rooms. Speak not of shotguns,
of ice picks, of mahogany incubi who mutter
beneath the mahogany stairs. Don't tell the nuns
I've said as much; worse, that you believe a word
the Old Growler says, lest you never end your

"voluntary commit," and linger in this glass-house,
chartless and over-pilled, beloved of St. Dymphna
alone, whom the stuttering priest, just back
from a dipsomaniacal tour of the Bronx, dubs,
"M-m-madhouse mistress of us all."

The Song from Moulin Rouge (1953)

On the Feast Day of my Birth, Da pulled me
from the weedy patch, swaddled me in cabbage leaves,

and snugged me, all bleary-eyed, into a produce box.
So proud, he rolled about town in his silver

Coupe de Ville and for an hour or-so, I was his
show-off joy, or *must* have been, for surely I

would sauce his spicy foot-longs, sizzle those
slap-patties, flipping them, fanning sliced cheese

like a cardsharp, my happy feet tapping before
the vats of hot grease, glad-hands scooping fries,

squirting mayo, and ring-a-dong-dinging the till.
Da believed this all before my first "swirly,"

before sliding rock-salt loads into the gray maw
of his scattergun, before knocking me to ground

with an axe handle behind the walk-in freezer,
before twenty years of rum shots and goofballs.

He didn't know the voices were singing for me—
the fulsome strings of Percy Faith and His Orchestra,

with Felicia Sanders warbling so sweetly, her sole
big hit, Number One that spring, played over again

on the Caddy's Motorola, the chorus swelling across
the diamond-tuck seats, glancing off the dash, sliding

around Da's slippery, misshapen smile, around
his Korea-issue aviator glasses and bomber jacket

and into the waxy box where I sang and sang along,
Where is your heart? O, where is your heart?

Nabokov at Big Da's Drive-In

Lycaeides melissa samuelis (Nabokov, 1944)

. . . Collected some special butterflies
today south of Topinabee.
—Diary, June 27, 1958

Dragging a damp rag along the counter, she
thinks *How strange the man with the silk gloves*
and butterfly net, seated at the picnic table
spooning frozen custard at his mouth,
the sweat at the brim of his Panama hat

beginning to cool, as hints of vanilla
rise from the dish. He spreads a Viennese
handkerchief across the pine tabletop,
opens an ancient marmalade jar,
and eases out dead butterflies,

gilt-edged along their tiny blue wings.
From a knapsack he pulls a largish pair
of tweezers and, in the sweet shade of the overhang,
nudges his specimens about, ordering them
first by size, next, by the slightest variance in tint.

The girl looks out across the graveled lot, dust rising
where a cherry-red Skyliner has pulled in
off Hatchery Road. Three boys are in the Ford,
the one in the back seat—*so cute!*—in his khaki
park uniform, the car's radio blasting out

the Andy Williams hit *Butterfly*.
She thinks of the film, a black-and-white,
Jack took her to last Saturday. A guy on the lam
meets a girl in a bar on a hot Hollywood night,
though the last reel unspools in a storm,

after the humongous snowblower churns over a thug—
his chipped flesh, we must believe, splattered,
all crimson and gristle, across the blizzarding field.
What she liked was the hot part, when Aldo Ray
bought Ann Bancroft a Mai Tai and said,

"I'll bet they've fluttered 'round since
you cut your second teeth." Meaning *what*, exactly?
The three boys approach her window, she slides
open her screen, leans, mariposal, into the light,
thinks, *Barbecues and coleslaw, betcha anything*,

as the strange man in the elegant white hat
and silk gloves scoops the last of his custard.
It was not the shaved ice of Lucerne,
Nabokov muses, infused with blackcurrant syrup,
but there is still a kilometer walk

to that pathetic rental flat, with its plug-less
icebox, its tar-paper kitchenette. The custard was cold
and the blue butterflies he so carefully spills
from his Viennese handkerchief
into the naphtha of his deadly marmalade jar
are *Remarkable. Fascinating.*

Slumgullion

> *Slumgullion* may not sound like the most appetizing name for a dish, but that's part of its charm. The word's etymology doesn't necessarily do it any favors: while the origins of *slumgullion* are somewhat murky, the word is believed to derive from *slum,* an old word for 'slime,' and *gullion,* an English dialectical term for 'mud' or 'cesspool' . . . The sense referring to the stew debuted a few decades later, and while there is no consensus on exactly what ingredients are found in it, that's the *slumgullion* that lives on today.
>
> —Merriam-Webster, "Did You Know?"

Maura Walsh, the organist at St. Mary's, taught Mam
to make this before I was born, back when Mam was
a month out of Mercywood and worked part-time
selling lilac water and rouge at Woolworth's.
Mam hadn't known *slumgullion.* What she knew
was a sort of goulash—ground beef, stewed tomatoes,
elbow macaroni—but Mrs. Walsh said if Mam
wanted to marry a marine sergeant like *she* had,
just back from Korea with a Bronze Star and fresh
rocker stripe, she'd need to give him some things
he hungered for, so Mam kept a recipe in the elegant
cursive of Mrs. Walsh. Yes, there was ground beef
but also potatoes, turnips, onions, carrots,
sometimes a wild leek, salt and pepper, perhaps a dash
of Italian parsley bought at DeBiasi's on Hupp Street,
beef stock, a little cornstarch to thicken, and if it were early
spring—often, this was made in spring—a bottle of bock beer
brewed in February, before Stroh's scrubbed the tanks;
brown, wicked-strong, and as close to Irish stout
as Mam was likely to get at a Kroger in mid-Michigan.
Everything was poured into a blue enameled stockpot
and simmered until dinner. Once, I walked home
from school, past the malt shop, the Shell station,
and the florist's, slipped in the side door and found Mam

passed out on the couch, a bucket of slumgullion
scorching on the stove. Those were days of New Maths,
but I could still count and knew enough to puzzle out
her secret: one empty bock for the stew, five empties
by the couch. And where was her whiskey?
I turned off the gas, covered her with the yellow
blanket, poured a bowl of Corn Pops, and snapped on
the Zenith to watch Heckle and Jeckle, those zany
Terrytoon magpies. I remember Jeckle saying
in a posh accent, "We cartoon characters can have
a wonderful life, if we only take advantage of it!" The rest
of that night was a romparoo, full of the usual high jinks.
Weeping, vomit, little seizures; a kind of madcap
hilarity ensued.

Slowdown

> Did you think Phil Levine was the only poet who ever worked at Kelsey-Hayes? Hell, the Jackson plant was crawling with poets and socialists.
>
> —J. D. Reed

Don't say that young Jim Gannon
tossed the open-end wrench
into the 80-ton Dreis & Krump press
on the third shift at Kelsey-Hayes
that September night in 1959,
or I'll have to fight you for it,
like I had to fight Ray Natschke,
the foreman's son, on the asphalt
playground across the street
from our parish school. No one can say
who threw that wrench and besides, it
was listed to Building 4, and Uncle Jim
hadn't been near the West Gate
in weeks. But when the highline stopped
and the Croats in the grind room
sat on their toolboxes, refusing to sweep,
someone whispered *Slowdown*
and soon there was a line of men
with their arms folded,
the baffled whoosh of the big
industrial fans, pushing silence
out the enormous chain-swivel windows,
and Ray Natschke's father, cursing
in German. Because it's of record
among the musty files, scattered
across the floor of a padlocked warehouse
in Detroit, let's say Uncle Jim was so lit
on fresh air and the Black Lake socialism
of Walter Reuther that from his belt

he pulled a Hohner Echo and began
to play the Irish songs taught him
as a child. He'd almost finished
Come Out, Ye Black and Tans when
Alphonse Natschke and his stooge boys
raised him by his elbows, dragged
him back among the palleted racks
of shiny black wheel hubs, gut-punched him
twice, and tossed him and his Echo
off the concrete loading dock. I can say
that at 4 am I was in the back
of Mam's dented Nash when my Uncle,
skinned to forehead-bone and spitting blood
from his pearly mouth, pulled out his
harmonica and played *The Rising of the Moon*
as Mam swerved through Loomis Street Park,
that he babbled and wept and splattered
the dash with blood, though Mam
slapped a towel at him and yelled *Stop it, Jimmy!*
As if a clean towel were enough, as if
this bloodiness might ever stop. I was
only 6. How could I know this would go on,
until Kelsey-Hayes was gone and the files were
gone and St. Mary's School, too? That it would go
on, long after Ray Natschke was dead, spleen-blown
across a muddy hole near Da Nang? Long after his father
pensioned out and spun his Chevy pickup
into a bridge abutment near St. Pete. Until even
poetry and the old songs were gone.
Can we circle now and recite a little poem
for this long line of dead men?
Can we slow down, rise from our chairs,
and sing the old songs with them?

Letter to Dowsie, from Roethke in Ireland

—St. Brigid's Psychiatric Hospital at Ballinasloe,
County Galway, September 3, 1960

Driven mad by channel wrack and fresh sprats in bad oil,
sobbing on the oyster dock, at lowest tide I was
rowed to the mail boat by a barefoot Carmelite,
then lugged ashore at Cleggan and poured into the back
of a Singer sedan. I swore I'd suppress my "affect"
for a splash on our way to the bughouse,
and the good padre, having tippled with me
in those dicey island days, found nothing against the faith
in that. He meted out *Kilbeggans* every six miles
or-so, toasting each chosen apostle, excluding the Iscariot,
but counting Matthias and Paul. As single-pot prodigal,
I've found an easier, softer way: drinking buttermilk,
noshing stewed apples and mealy fishcakes
with the daft nuns and my attending physician,
a kindly man who's the spitball image of Barry Fitzgerald.
Walrus-like, I've wallowed in the hydro baths
as in our famous days at Mercywood, and thanks
to my transatlantic laurels, my benzo-calm,
and affable demeanor, I'm driven to a public house
on *seisiún* nights aboard the moron-bus—allowed
a few stiff drinks and recitation of a poem.
It's grand to hush the fiddles and part a cloud of pipe smoke,
led through the tavern door by four orderlies in white,
as if I'm blind O'Carolan, stumbled home at last,
escorted by that squadroon of virtuous angels
by which minor deities are ushered into the world.
On the wall chart of temperaments, mine approaches a shaker
of dry martinis—*sanguine* with ice and three drops of *melancholic.*
Dowsie, when did you last climb a honeysuckle trellis?
When did you last scurry through an asylum greenhouse,

tripping over clay pots and hashing your knees?
I imagine you now as sea-lioness, sleek and black,
your most clever pup dropped carelessly,
left to gorge on red dulse in a midnight sea,
and you, shrieking all those long tumultuous hours
atop a granite rock, eelgrass wilding beyond you in the surf.

Crash Injures Six Children; Two Serious

—*The Jackson Citizen Patriot,*
Sunday, August 6, 1961

Does no one recall Saturday mornings
and the name of the show after *Sky King*,
just before *Game of the Week*? The professor
and a cop rolling deadlies across the screen—

pointing out crumpled Buicks and Fords,
tolling lost arms, amazed at the corpse
found grinning in the huckleberries,
how his high-tops caught the bumper

and the body-was-dragged-this-far.
It could've been avoided, they said, all so
safe had the salesman not guzzled five *Jacks*
at a blind pig, had the troubled teen

not been humping the clutch for pink slips,
had the pretty cheerleader, with a prom king
to die for, grasped the meaning of S-T-O-P,
the concept of *These tires have no tread.*

We were spooning Rice Krispies; that snap
crackle pop drowned in powdered milk,
all of us nestled at our black-and-white Zenith,
laying down our bowls, our spoons,

hiding moon-pie faces with tiny hands,
peeking through fingers as the music began
and the doomed coupe swept down the death-ramp.
We'd yell *Slow down!* and *Watch out!* But always

that *Looney Tunes*, don't-look-now, songbird-
in-the-sky camera work; a glide path of regret—
the crash and silence, a stunned wailing,
then sirens and hissy flares, the gored bodies

and weepy next-of-kin, the bloody stolen lives!
And what if God had slowed a second or-so
as Mam's Nash roared off to the Green Stamps
Redemption Center? God recalling

a double play from the Tigers' game, for God sees
precisely, not as a dim umpire—a slow roller
to second, Jake Wood toes the bag, leaps high
over Skowron's take-out slide, and fires

to Cash at first. C'mon, we all know
what happened in '61! Was Yogi safe or out?
And for those lost seconds, for the Lord's
jolly baseball reverie, the crash *hadn't*—

no fatal swerve, no careening across yellow lines,
no deer paused at crest of the road
to sniff peaches at blush in a rolly-polly field,
and the death cars missing, each by inches,

the DeSoto's irate driver yelling, *Christ, lady,*
watch where you're going! And Mam oblivious,
smiling, merciful God! All her kids apoplectic
but alive, ducking below the dash as Mam speeds on,

yelling *Shut up! Shut up!* Laughing and tippling
gin-and-Tang from her double-cupped, upside-down
witch-hat Dixie cup.

The Feast of St. Blaise

> Through the intercession of St. Blaise, bishop and martyr,
> may God deliver you from every disease of the throat
> and from every other illness: In the name the Father,
> and of the Son, and of the Holy Spirit.

At the close of mass, before Sister Bridget
trudged us back to the mysteries of line segments

and failure at the New Maths, we were called to the rail
so Monsignor Hardy might press two candles

across our necks and mumble the blessing
of St. Blaise, said to have yanked a thousand fishbones

from the throats of choking orphans,
before turning them loose with empty hands

to the zany dark of the fourth century.
I could taste this blessing like a cherry lozenge,

sparing me from croup, from strep and thrush,
from cankers of cheek and gum,

from an inside pitch sent whizzing below my chin,
from the drunken whacks and throttles

of Da's fists, when I, so damn goofy, forgot to fork
through Friday's baked fish and began to choke

on a stickle of pin-bones. This was before Heimlich
and his sweet moves, when all that might save me

from Da's sudden curse and whiskeyed hands
were candles, looped with shiny ribbons,

and a knack for scuttling, blue-faced
and breathless, inches below a thrown fist.

How I loved to duck and weave; to dodge his Bluto-style
Ka-pows, as I gagged on pollock and lima beans

and stumbled for the coal bin, where I walloped my back
against the gummy black wall, teaching myself to cough it

all up, learning to live my twentieth-century life.

Child atop a Half-Constructed Root Beer Stand, Swamping Hot Tar

—after Theodore Roethke

Sweat gluing my shorts to my skinny legs.
My Chuck Taylor shoes leaving the starry marks
of Chuck's sole across the tar-papered roof.
Three buckets of stinky hot tar staring up like accusers.
Six bags of pea gravel to be thrown across pools
of hot tar, once tar is poured and slopped and spread.
Windless, and no white clouds rushing anywhere.
Not far, not far at all, a tangle of cedars shade trout
stalking *caddis* through the rum-tumble rocks
of a mystery river. A current I can almost hear
babbling below the desultory traffic.
And no one, no one I actually know pointing up
and shouting, "You're too close to that edge!
Watch out! For Chrissake, kid, don't fall!"

Destination Moon

> According to legend, the peony emanated from the moon. Its glossy seeds supposedly shine through the night too, offering protection from devils, nightmares, and other terrors of darkness. Known as "the blessed rose," the peony also purportedly guarded against illness, injury, and insanity. The superstitious wore beads, carved from the flower's roots, as amulets. They harvested those roots at night, since woodpeckers were thought to jealously guard the peony by day—and to peck out the eyes of anyone caught interfering with the plant.
>
> —Audrey Stallsmith, "Moonstruck Peony" (2013)

> Now, let's pretend that umbrella of yours is a shotgun!
>
> —Narrator to Woody Woodpecker
> in *Destination Moon* (1950)

i.

Crazy Mam falls from the battered Nash
to the peonies along the drive.
Crazy Mam is drunk. She is sick.
She is crawling through peonies,
lurching among the blooms,
vomiting at the flowers, breaking
stems, slurring, scattering petals, shouting
that her goddam kids made her drink
highballs all day at the clip joint.
From the window of the playroom,
above the drive and bruised peonies,
on the Morning Glory side of the bungalow,
her angels call out, *Crazy Mam,*
what's wrong? Why are you sick?
Can't you see? I whisper to her angels,
we are her goddam kids. We make her sick,
we make her drink highballs all day!
We sent her to the clip joint! Crazy Mam,
was it Tuesday we hurt you, watching that
TV show about monkeys in space capsules,
as we ate bananas, raisin toast with cinnamon

and sugar, and you sat there with your puzzle-
piece face, pushing it around your achy head?
Or was it today, as Miss Junie Sunlight
warmed our beds? The Morning Glories
popped, the peonies were fat. We slept in—
so cozy! But woke to a trail of space tinsel
and beer nuts sprinkled across the dead-nettle,
you and the battered Nash, already in orbit,
already gone to the finger-snappin' clip joint.

ii.

Now Crazy Mam crawls to the depths
of her garden, crushing the peonies,
scaring her angels. And the ants that bite
and bite, that love the nectar of her peonies,
that feast upon that sweetness, fall in a tumbly
shower onto Crazy Mam's pretty hair; they fall
across her back. The ants are falling, cart-
wheeling, as Crazy Mam begins to scream—
ants, crawling across her legs and back!
She rolls among the broken peony stems,
among the green leaves, among the scattering petals
and bitey ants, wailing at what the angels
have done. And then it was there interposed
between her goddam angels and the wrecked
peony bed, a strange bird—crimson-head,
ebony feathers, white trim. A big bird, a bird
as crazy as Crazy Mam. It's Woody Woodpecker!
That's not nice Woody, though.
It's flat-top Woody, stout-legged Woody,
cigar-chomping Woody. It's *Hurry up!*
Let's-win-this-goddam-war! Woody. It's Woody,
painted on the nose of a Thunderbolt, during the bloody
last days of WWII. It's 40-cal. Woody, diving
low over the so-sorry streets of Bremen—
Ack! Ack! Ack! Now, Crazy Woody

joins the ants, diving from the leaky roof
of the bungalow, buzzing at Crazy Mam's
pretty hair, at her rheumy eyes.
The woodpecker fills the yard with rattle calls,
with angry, querulous churrs; carving
stunts and taunts and barrel rolls, as Crazy Mam
wipes her face and wags a finger in the sky.

iii.

Where is that shotgun? Crazy Mam needs
to know. She says she will shoot
goddam Woody, she will blast the ants,
she will shoot the goddam angels, too! But she
will never find the shotgun. I hid the shotgun
in the storm cellar. I dragged it up high and hid
it lengthwise behind the dusty canned tomatoes,
after Big Da went MIA. The ants biting
you, and Woody, who has not yet had a taste;
they already know there is no sweetness in you,
Crazy Mam. There are only highballs
and beer nuts. And shotgun shells, 12 gauge,
rattling 'round the pockets of your blue bathrobe.
Who besides me knows this, has fondled them?

iv.

Crazy Mam, crawl for the battered Nash!
Pull yourself up by the doorframe! the angels might
shout, were they older, if they knew what a doorframe
was, were they not so afraid. But the angels
are quiet. They watch from the playroom—from
among the Lincoln Logs, the hairless dolls, a jump-
jump horse, a scatter of Tinker Toys, and a picture book
of outer space, with rockets lifting off and bright
nose-cones, with meteors and sparkly tail comets
whizzing by—and say no more. The youngest
squeeze their eyes shut, they put their little hands over

their big ears. They have already seen, have already heard
that shotgun go off—chasing away a scabby cat,
blowing out windows (Ka-boom!) in the so-sorry garage.
Who could blame your angels, for wanting
to steal bananas and raisin bread, cinnamon and sugar,
for wanting to climb high into the battered Nash,
for blasting off like space monkeys, to circle
and loop and slingshot away from the horseshoe magnet
of earth's gravity—Destination Moon—for wanting
to peek back upon you from a deep crater, to see
this strange woman who hates them and would kill them,
to look down upon your biting ants and the furious diving bird,
upon your ruined peonies and decrepit bungalow
and shake their heads *No, No,* for days, for light-years,
for half a century, until every bit of you in them
dies and disappears?

The Nazarene

> If there be a prophet among you, I the Lord will make myself known unto him in a vision, and will speak to him in a dream.
>
> —NUMBERS 12:11

Now Mam hates her peonies
and stalks their nodding heads
with machete and whiskey jar, slashing,
roiling the air with stems,
with whirled petals and maledictions.
Not enough, she decides, to heap and burn
the flower-heads, the petals, and leaves.
She must take her trowel and bucket, dig
and scrape the peonies—roots and tubers
and eyes. Every fuzzy tendril must be
torn from the bed of her garden.
So she begins, wandering through the slashed
green stems, sweating, sipping from her
bottomless jar, working against whiskey
and the cicada-drills of Thursday afternoon.
Then, as if the Nazarene, laden with miracles,
comes a Black man in worn overalls
and chambray shirt, pushing a gray barrow,
in which rattle a hoe, a rake, and shovel.
The Black man toes his shovel deep
into the grass. Yes, Ma'am, he will
dig out her peony bed; blossom, tendril,
root, and bulb, haul away stems
and make flat the earth; an afternoon's work,
for $10 cash and the peony roots.
And this he does, sweating the tall hours
with sharp tools; pulling roots, shaking
clots of loamy dirt, while Mam watches
from the porch swing, smiling and drinking,

liking the artful ways this Black man digs,
until she says, "That's enough, now.
Come on up for a drink."
He collects his $10 cash (Mam counts
each dollar bill to his great hand), nodding
and Yes, Ma'am-ing in his big voice, drinking
only ice water, until Mam is slurring words,
babbling of Ozzie Virgil at third base, of
Orval Faubus and bad times in Little Rock,
of toothless Governor Earl Long
holding court at the *Sazerac* with Blaze Starr
in spangled tow; until Mam nods and slow-blinks
away. The Black man looks at my forehead,
my raccoon eyes, still purple-black
from when a Model A pickup, handbrake
not set, an oar wedged in its bed, rolled
down an incline and banged Mam's old Nash,
the whorled grip of the oar hitting me
kneeling in the backseat, staring out the open window—
wood to skull, like a thing ordained;
like the finger-touch of God.
Odd, how the whole while I'd seen the pickup,
driverless, that oar lodged in the truck-bed,
the angle of their descent, but did not turn away.
And the Nazarene, whom I'd squinted to watch
all afternoon in the steamy hot light,
his Black hands calmly digging peony roots
and laying them as baby corpses in his gray barrow,
his body lit by my concussion's shimmering
gold auras—how, years later, as in a dream,
I saw him in a watercolor by Blake; was it a study
for *Pity*? A dark rider aglow, flying by
on a wingéd horse, stretched earthward to swoop
the child from the arms of its cataleptic mother—
this Black man smiles and says, "Best nudge up
your momma and lead her to the couch."

That fall, I saw him again near the Drive Thru
at Polly's, selling his repotted peonies
from his gray barrow—60¢ a waxy carton,
pre-fertilized, and sure to bloom next summer.
My bruises were as yellow curry, the swelling . . .
I no longer saw astonishing light around the body
of anyone and when I asked the Black man if he
remembered me, he shook his head and said,
"Sorry, son, I've never known you before or since."

Blue Racer

—Coluber constrictor foxii

I saw a blue racer
flicker through the candle-weed
and wanting it—
cream belly and cobalt flanks,
a darting tongue with quick tip—
I snatched it as a raptor might:
blue dazzler, eyed once and swept high.
I placed it in a wooden box
[the "fastest snake" astonished, writhing]
and laid the box between the wheels
blocked high beneath a stripped-out Nash.
And there, the serpent would not calm,
wanting only dew on its quick-tipped tongue,
wanting to be gone. It was a wicked sin
to keep a racer boxed beneath a salvage wreck.
But those were days of wanton needs;
of covetousness. Each morning,
beguiled by the electric blue,
greedy for its coiling, for its cold blink
as I cracked the box to sunlight,
for the serpent's power, alive and sly
beneath the wretched Nash, to make Mam curse
in her whiskey-addled tongue;
all this consoled me into autumn,
until I found the box shattered
and the snake tossed among the Queen Anne's lace,
hacked to cream and cobalt pieces.
Its head was stepped flat
as foretold, and there was that scythe—
wet blade plunged into sand.
Who killed the blue racer?

Not I, not even in an angry boy's dream,
though I'd slept fitfully that night,
though there'd been a stalking moon
and a man whistling high through the tall pines,
though the book said a troublesome child
would stir and stir, causing the serpent's death.
And oh, those blow flies got on with it—
that grievous sipping; their cutty
little tongues. So eagerly they flew
to their long-anointed tasks.

Early at Big Da's Drive-In

His compassions are new every morning.
—Lamentations 3:22–23

Sitting at the picnic table under the orange canopy
counting cars drifting off the expressway;
tourists on their way to Mackinac Island, the UP,
even our state park—"Left at the blinking light,
go a half mile down the old highway."
Da's in the kitchen, step-laddered at the soft-serve
with the woman who opens six days a week
(Sundays she sings for the Methodists),
showing her again what she already knows—
how to unseal the creamy mix, pour it into the machine,
and snap the "ON" toggle in time to freeze by noon.
I'm staying out of Da's sight.
When he finds me, I'll fill the steam table
with hot dogs and coney sauce, top off the ketchups, etc.
Before lunch hour, I'll stamp sixty pounds
of ground beef into hamburger patties, cut
two dozen fryers into Da's famous Chubby Chicken—
you cleave a chicken into nine pieces and the backbone disappears!
I could show you how, if you'd like. But why start early?
I'm still counting cars. Some are leaving town.
Next week, gin-looped and whiskey jaggéd,
Da will break my nose with a hamburger spatula,
black my left eye, and "cut off" the money
he was never going to pay me,
because I'm leaving at the end of August
to go back to school. He'll call me an "ungrateful bastard,"
smack me again, and say worse. Beyond the north canopy
the sandpipers scoot about the half-lit morning field,
piper-ing, obsessed with their scrabbled-up

nests (nimble-grass, little stones, gum wrappers),
dancing a frantic broken-wingéd dance
should a carrion bird, soaring over the pines,
suddenly drop from flight.

Missing Woman Found Alive in Quarry

—*The Straitsland Resorter,* June 25, 1973

She was going to mass at St. Monica's
with a fifth of *Tullamore* and a go-cup of ice
scoured from the sputtery ice machine,
when darkness took her. Who knew where
she might run? We saw her bottom-out
the resurrected Nash—she'd sworn she would die
in it—whirl gravel at the restaurant drive,
then turn the county road toward Afton,
lofting over the Michigan Central,
up the Sandy, and past the rickety fire tower.
For hours, that's all we knew. Beyond the icy
Pigeon River, Mam turned left instead of right—
she *must* have—wheeled north, then swerved
down a two-track, through brackens and jack pines.
She flatted an arrow daubed on plywood
and launched from the cut of the limestone quarry,
airborne some thirty feet out, out over
the green water—so far out, my brother proposed
a Family Puzzler: How fast was Mam traveling
when the drive wheels of that two-ton Nash
lost touch with the quarry rim? With proofs to be
written as limericks, wax-sealed in manila fold-ups
for however long it took, and read at Mam's wake.
Who dreamed she would live another forty-eight years?
It was a dust year, the summer of grass fires,
the quarry pond was low and the Nash sank
only to its adjustable mirrors; no deeper.
Before sunset, we found her—sullen, unhurt,
seated atop the swoopy roof, rafted among the water lilies
and damsel flies, the bluegills and punkies stippling

the quiet pond. She stared at the fractured walls
and gravel shoals of the quarry, like a cursed woman
in some Pre-Raphaelite canvas, leaning into the day's
last light; almost, it seemed, poised to weep a desolate
question from the thwarts of her sad craft
or, as Mam might have once believed,
almost ready, *bel canto*, to sing.

Elegy with Blue-Handled Filet Knife

—August 26, 1974

The day she dropped me still bleeding
in Ann Arbor—fall semester, my duffel bag

jammed in back, we went to Drake's for cold limeade
and Mam bought a double to-go, because

she'd stashed a pint of *Mohawk* under the driver's
seat to brace her for the trip back north.

She knew I was never going back
to Da's orange-and-brown hot dog stand,

not after Monday night, when he slammed me
against the fryer over a spilled order of onion rings

and kept coming like a Kerry bull
because I wasn't worth a good-goddam

and I thought of the blue-handled filet knife
I'd slicked across a honing stone

just before the dinner rush, the blade
blood-warm in four inches of sudsy water,

and pulled myself to the stainless-steel sink—
splash sizzling across the black grill—backing off

her snorting man, eyes wide, circling the prep table,
until an angel of a sane and better nature

whispered No, you're gone tomorrow
and three hundred miles south; over limeade

in the calm of Drake's Sandwich Shop
you'll hear her say she loves you, for the first time

in your pathetic life, if you stumble out the back door
now, hide all night in the jack pine woods,

and do not stab her man.

In Search of a Drinkie, Mam Sneaks Out of Assisted Living to Visit *The Blue Merrow*

> According to Gaelic legend, the Merrow frolicked in the frigid waters near the rugged Irish coastline . . . these sea fairies were women from the waist up, and fish from the waist down.
>
> —Ciara O'Brien

She dreams of Bobby Darin and *Beyond the Sea*, always just a nickel on the Rock-Ola, with Peggy Lee's *How Deep is the Ocean?* the next play. It isn't hard to slip past a nurse during shift change, and aboard her three-wheeled Mobil-o she is free in the October dark to visit Connie the bartender and Rick the smiling bar-back. She knows Rick can lift her from the Mobil-o to an orbiting captain's chair at the flame-oak bar, tugged all the way from Cape May, New Jersey, by Gerry himself in '59. She was there the day the flat-bed showed up, a green tarp stretched tight across the swirling wood. "What you gonna do with that?" she asked Gerry, who rolled his eyes and shook out a vodka gimlet.

She is cruising down Seaway Drive, singing Julie London's *Cry Me a River*, the Mobil-o's battery half-charged and no prowl cars in sight—no midnight joggers, no bread trucks idling at the big bakery. She whirrs past a possum sniffing an oily go-bag. The possum flops, throws a paw, feigning "possum death," and she thinks of Phil O'Day, the shorthand teacher she used to meet at the *Merrow* most Friday afternoons for school gossip and whiskey sours. How he'd follow her home and collapse on her davenport, a wet hand-towel, folded, laid flat above his oversized black glasses, cooling his forehead, calming his 80-proof ululations, until his breath slowed, steadied, until he fell asleep.

She hungers for drink-noise and a crock of cheese; cubed ice, the smoky bite of bar mix (peanuts, tiny pretzels, little rounds of hard rye-bread), the frothy grasshoppers, the daiquiris, even a jigger or-so of *Wild Turkey*, straight-up with a branch-water back, whenever the mood suited her, after Phil laid down his *KOOL*, pulled her from her chair for a foxtrot to *Sea of Love*, as Connie clapped hands for the cozy twosome, then comped the next round, "Top-shelf, kids; no well drinks." Maybe Phil can meet her tonight.

But when Mam rolls—silent, stealthy—into the drive, there are no lot-lights, no *Fresh Perch* sign, no fish tank aglow with neon tetras, no side-lit red door. There are only cracked blacktop, a smashed beer bottle, a rectangle of weedy dirt where the bar once stretched, and stars and moonlight and box elder leaves, falling. She does not remember that Connie is dead, Phil is dead, Rick's doing a hard dime in Ionia; that Gerry cashed out before the fire and retired down near Weeki Wachee Springs, where on Sunday afternoons he limps to the Famous Mermaid Show, to see the sweet young girls who dive and kick their pastel tails through the vodka-like waters, who roll, who tumble and draw deep breaths from the bubbling air hose, who exhale, and who will never drown.

The Coney Island Translations

Thank God, I speak in tongues more than any of you.
—1 CORINTHIANS 18:18

Hexagenia limbata

After long silence, I call my father in ICU
and speak to his charge nurse. She says
he is resting but rings me through.
My Father, holy-carded, blessed, so anointed
now, mutters along in a nonsense-tongue—
undulant, a fogged soundscape of low trills
and sleepy sonorants and at a stagy lull,
in the just-heard flow of a nymph-laden river—
unfledged, so-tired of sliding over stones.

He coughs once, and I hear his flukey liver.
He coughs again and I hear the bile,
the gruel-thick blood, clotting at his spleen.
And then, though I feared this, in syllables
and fricatives, in mumbled glyphs and fractals
of speech, his words, their dark tangle-fall,
come slowly upon me—the Frankish,
the hot dog Greek of Corinthians and Acts,
the Gaelic of failure and whiskey-bred anomie.

I hear some of the Great Lakes farm boy,
touching pencil-lead to tongue, scrawling bad
advice on when to plow the muck-field,
of the buck private, deployed to pack lettuce
in dreary Stockton, as his regiment sailed off
to medals and death on Saipan. I hear, yes,
something about "Abbas" and "a great wind"
and now fully comes the fearsomeness of God—
a raptor's talons grasping my shoulders,

the Spirit's gray infested wings vastly moving
the staticky air, and a blue flame rising,
as of a great iris, as of a fire-ring set on high, hissing
propane-blue beneath a galvanized steam-table,
and at last, I know my Father is passing on
the secrets of his Coney Island hot dogs—
Listener, we keep such secrets!—the snap-skin
franks, two pounds of browned hamburger,
tomato paste, salt, sweet cumin, and chili spice.

But Father, I say, I already know this.
It was beaten into me through days and nights
at your blaze-orange hot dog stand, from
dawn through the all-night mayfly hatches,
the *Hex* risen from water, whirling at every lot-light,
at canopy light, at every high-beam, endlessly
rising for the fat yellow moon, the duns
free-popping and their spinners, falling, slicking
your lot with egg sacs and spawned-out husks,
as the tires of pickup trucks spun donuts
and flattened whatever detritus was left behind—
the emptied mayflies, go-bags, drink cups,
french fries, coney boats—and crushed it all
to the bitumen of your weepy, chlorinated gravel.
Father, the *Hex* would do what they'd come to do
and die. You, furious, could not stop them.

And I, ever the prodigal son, finally
toss the phone, drop, and roll away the flames
that scorch my forehead, before your secret is
truly told, in whatever hellish tongue
you always felt called to speak—your shotgun,
your knot-lashed belt, the machete-cut hawthorn
switch, the welts, my slap-blooded mouth,
your unholy names for me, even your silence—
each of these a lifelong curse and none a blessing,

your story told in a voice so dark, so baffling,
it has taken me these seven lucky years
to translate, to speak again, to finally
wrestle your drunken, dead, night-angel body
to a heaving draw, to re-call you but once, Father, out
of this deep, deaf Coney Island sadness
and ask for you by name.

To Tell the Hornets

—Dolichovspula norwegica

Mother, after your death, may I
raise a ladder beneath the stave oak
with its great parchment nest
and, as the hornets come and go,
climb among them, tell them you
are gone, so hornets leaving the nest
might hurry among the carcasses
of the lost, whispering at the whorls
of their dead ears, warning of what
is to come. And those in flight, once
safely home—antennae in orbit,
swarmed, gathered at the vespiary
gate—might speed the combed maze
to the Queen herself, and say, Oh,
your Sister is gone, Lovely One,
in the stilted manner of hornets
that, once each nest-year, belies all
fierceness. With the news fully
told, may all who so choose, hiss
round my head, stinging my hands,
my heart, all swollen with their venom,
everywhere, dizzy with their stings,
as I drape black mourning cloth
and tie blue bottles high among the boughs
of the hornet tree, knowing it is fall
and soon, the foundress must drop from
her pesthouse, and crawl without ado
beneath the red leaves and chipped bark,
to rest and to rest—for such is always
the real work of the dead.

Bull Thistles

—Cirsium vulgare

I never saw a wild thing sorry for itself.
—D. H. Lawrence

Da comes with pool cue, his cutting torch, with a 12 gauge, with a brickbat, with a monkey wrench, with a tire iron, with a Bowie knife, with bayonet, with a candlestick, with brass knuckles. He sights-in, takes aim, scrambles from the gravel pit, from a grinding cement churn, kicks loose, and rappels down the abandoned fire tower. He rises from weedy lakes, gnashes teeth in cedar swamps, from snags deep in the crooked bends of green rivers, blinking with dead eyes, with his list, for a reckoning, for immolation, with metal chaff, with sputtering flak, with blackjacks, with bandoliers, with a full clip, locked-and-loaded, with tracers, with hollow points, pressing my fingers to his whirring slicer, mashing my hands into hamburger patties, dead beneath the hammer of a forty-ton press, my legs splayed beneath his brush hog, exhaust pipes charring flesh, in an abandoned salt mine, dog-paddling deep in the ladder-less cistern, sprinkled with quick-lime, dead—drowned in the November suck of Lake Superior waves, in chain-lightning along the river road, dropped by a crush of buzz-sawn trees. He lurks below the skin of the pond, among lily pads, reaching from muck to pull me down, drag me under, until I stir, flutter-wake, or seem to—in a dustbowl, in a great American desert, beneath a Lawrence Tree looking up, its limbs like great twisty creeks of blood, all feeding a great curved trunk of blood, sucking life from the blue lakes of its crown and the white stars scattered beyond, until I truly wake, to a memory of Da half a century ago, his shovel, its whorled handle hard against my temple, knocking me down, and Da stabbing at my scuttling body with his shovel-blade, cursing, spittle flying from his twisted mouth, Da stabbing, hacking at earth as I reel back, body raking across thorns, across needled stems, across the leaves and jagged pinks of bull thistles, and scrambling from these and rising, hands pushing up from thistles and away, shovel across my back again, and running, blooded with a broken nose, with bloody ear, with great wounds and tiny wounds, cuts that were never bandaged, wounds that have not been salved, that fester, with slivers and tiny spears near invisible, that have not come free, that have never dissolved, that will never work loose—out of that colonial boy's palms, up through his flayed and prickly skin.

Deus ex Machina

> A *deus ex machina* will never appear in real life
> so you best make other arrangements.
> —MARISHA PESSL, *SPECIAL TOPICS IN CALAMITY PHYSICS* (2006)

Within a pastel Tilt-a-Whirl,
all spinning-dizzy teacups, the carnies take
their smirking turns, astonishing the virgins.

This—coming to know centrifugal force—
was a tale of my '50s. Afterwards
came heavy water, Dagmar, and the long betrayal
of the Rosenbergs. Don't worry.

Pythagoras said, *Above the clouds*
and their shadows, shines a star with its light.
Ergo, each right triangle whispers the story
of Tobias, with God at his Pole Star
jacking the clutch, and Raphael in-irons, at the furthest point
of the hypotenuse—rapturous,
dragging celestial chains along the beach.

Avast, me Hearties!

Endless this infinity, because there simply is no end!
At the ill you have done, Lord, be troubled
and rejoice in the good. Above the droughty field,

beyond the Jack Yeats blues of the loll-headed chicory,
piratic crows wheel and fall upon the corn.

Notes

"Because I Wish to Avoid Extravagant Claims . . .": *The Informer* (1935) was directed by John Ford and starred Victor McLaglen. The film is based on the novel *The Informer* by Liam O'Flaherty (1925). McLaglen won a Best Actor Academy Award for his portrayal of Gypo Nolan, a disgraced IRA operative who informs to the British regarding the whereabouts of a wanted member of the IRA, in return for funds to buy passage from Ireland to the United States. In addition to McLaglen's Oscar, *The Informer* won three other Academy Awards: Best Director for John Ford, Best Adapted Screenplay for Dudley Nichols, and Best Score for Max Steiner. *Babaí* is an Irish word for *baby.*

***"Portrait of a Woman between 1948 and 1949"*:** The painting by the African American painter Hughie Lee-Smith (1915–1999) is in the permanent collection of the Detroit Institute of Arts. The actual title of the painting is *Portrait of a Woman*, and the dates of its creation are given by the artist as "between 1948 and 1949." I have taken the liberty of combining this information into an "alternative" title for the poem. "Eloise" was the designated postal address of the Wayne County General Hospital facility located in what is now Westland, Michigan. In its various iterations, the facility was generally known as the Eloise Psychiatric Hospital (1839–1982). During the Depression, more than ten thousand residents lived at Eloise, on over nine hundred acres with over two thousand staff members. In addition to a psychiatric care hospital, the complex included a tuberculosis sanatorium, a poor house, and medical facilities for the poor. It also housed displaced industrial workers following the end of World War II.

***"Angela Sweets, Black Pearls, Columbia Stars"*:** *Weán* is a Gaelic term for a young child.

"Burning Out the Redwings": The tactics for controlling redwing blackbirds recorded in this poem are extremely dangerous and should not be attempted under any circumstances. In addition, the killing of redwing blackbirds is prohibited by the Migratory Bird Treaty Act of 1918, 16 USC Sections 703–12.

"Jack Kennedy Whistle-Stops . . .": On October 14, 1960, at approximately 2 a.m., John F. Kennedy proposed the establishment of the Peace Corps in a speech before some ten thousand students on the steps of the Michigan

Union, on the campus of the University of Michigan in Ann Arbor. A historic marker at the main entrance to the Michigan Union records this event. Later that morning, Kennedy spoke to a smaller crowd from a train-car platform at the rail station in Jackson, Michigan, thirty-five miles west, then continued on his whistle-stop tour across the state. The song "Don't Worry Baby" by Brian Wilson, with lyrics by Roger Christian, drew upon the Ronette's 1963 hit "Be My Baby" and, as noted in the poem, was not written as of the date of Kennedy's whistle-stop tour across southern Michigan. "Don't Worry Baby" appeared on the Beach Boys' album *Shut Down, Volume 2*, released in March 1964. With regard to the cigar plot and other efforts to assassinate Fidel Castro, see *Executive Action: 634 Ways to Kill Fidel Castro* by Fabio Escalante (Ocean Press, 2006).

***"Experts Hope to Blow Out Oil Fire on Tuesday"*:** Paul Neal "Red" Adair (1915–2004) was an Irish American oil well firefighter. He employed innovative techniques to extinguish and cap oil well fires and blowouts, both land-based and offshore. The John Wayne film *Hellfighters* (1968) directed by Andrew Victor McLaglen (1920–2014), the son of actor Victor McLaglen, was loosely based on events in Adair's life and firefighting career. The Garfield Farley oil well fire near Albion, Michigan, began on February 26, 1962, and was extinguished by Red Adair on March 2, 1962.

"I'm Never Told of Family Funerals": Lourdes is a small town in the Pyrenees Mountains in southwestern France. Lourdes is said to have been the site of as many as eighteen visitations by the Blessed Virgin Mary in 1858, as witnessed by a young girl, Bernadette Soubirous (later canonized as Saint Bernadette of Lourdes). The town became a Marian shrine, and the faithful often go there in search of miracles, including medical cures. Jonas Edward Salk (1914–1995) was an American virologist and medical researcher. On April 12, 1955, it was announced at the University of Michigan School of Public Health that Salk had created a clinically effective vaccine for the prevention of infantile paralysis (polio).

"That Fall": During the 1950s, a number of secret military devices were installed and tested in Michigan's Upper Peninsula in an effort to provide advanced warning of a possible Soviet air or missile attack on the United States. In many instances, Western Electric Company (then a subsidiary of AT&T) was contracted to develop and install these devices.

"St. Brendan and the Foaming Sea **(1964)"** imagines a child's response to a grade-school art contest sponsored by the Irish government as part of its exhibition at the 1964 World's Fair in New York City. The Irish Pavilion was dedicated on May 16, 1964, by John Lynch, Ireland's minister for industry and commerce. During the dedication, Lynch said, "We chose this day because it is the Feast of Saint Brendan, who was the first Irishman to reach the New World, long before the coming of Columbus." Saint Brendan the Navigator (c. 484–577 AD) is said to have made a seven-year voyage to "Paradise" with a group of his monks (c. 512–530 AD). This journey is recorded in *The Voyage of Saint Brendan: Journey to the Promised Land* (c. 900 AD) and other sources. The record of his journey supports the Irish claim that it was Saint Brendan, rather than Columbus, who discovered the New World.

"Turnips": *Cosúlacht* is an Irish word meaning *likeness*.

"To Recite the Mysteries": Though no longer made in the United States, Mars bars continue to be produced in Great Britain. The verses quoted are based on Psalms 77:2 and Lamentations 1:1, respectively.

"Cotton House Fire": The cotton storehouse at the Pepperell Cotton Mill in Biddeford, Maine, caught fire on the evening of October 29, 1915, and burned through the next day. Losses and damages were estimated to be in excess of $500,000 in 1915 dollars (approximately $15.7 million in 2024 dollars). No specific cause was ever determined for the fire, though some suspected arson.

"*The State of Maine*": In 1918, Camp Devens in Massachusetts was one of the principal staging grounds for the US war effort in World War I. On September 1, its barracks were jammed with forty-five thousand Army soldiers waiting to be shipped to France. By the end of September, Camp Devens had become one of the most significant infection points of the Spanish flu pandemic: More than fifteen thousand soldiers came down with influenza at Camp Devens, and more than eight hundred of them died. Family and friends from nearby communities who visited soldiers at the facility carried the Spanish flu home with them and spread it throughout New England and the mid-Atlantic.

"Annie Kelly, 25": The Central Maine Sanitarium at Atwood Mountain near Fairfield (founded in 1910 and under state control from 1915 until its closure in 1970) treated tuberculosis patients with advanced cases of the disease. In sanatariums of that time, an effort was made to serve attractive and nourishing meals on good china and with quality glassware and silverware. It was hoped that good food and table service would encourage the appetites of the tuberculosis patients, which were often suppressed by the disease.

"Among the 796 Dead Children . . .": The Bon Secours Mother and Baby Home (1925–1961) in the town of Tuam, County Galway, Ireland, was a maternity home for unmarried mothers and their children operated by the Bon

Secours Sisters, an order of Catholic nuns. Excavations carried out between November 2016 and February 2017 established that an estimated 796 babies and young children who died at the facility had been secretly interred in an underground septic tank located on the site.

"Dowsie Gannon, Age 2, in Cleveland": The *20th Century Limited* was a luxury express train that operated between New York City and Chicago from 1902 until 1967. The phrase "red-carpet treatment" is said to be derived from its passengers' use of a specially designed red carpet to walk to the train when boarding. The train was a principal setting of the film *20th Century* (1934), directed by Howard Hawks and starring John Barrymore and Carole Lombard. The film is often cited as a prototype for Hollywood's "screwball comedies."

"Last Letter from Great-Aunt Nora Gannon . . .": Bill Gannon (1902–1965) was a prominent member of the Irish Republican Army (IRA) and later a founding member of the Communist Party of Ireland. On July 10, 1924, along with fellow militants Archie Doyle and Timothy Coughlin, he assassinated Kevin O'Higgins, the justice minister of the Irish Free State, in an attack along the Boostertown Road near Dublin. The assassins considered O'Higgins, who had authorized the hanging of seventy-seven IRA members held in Irish custody, to be a traitor to the Irish cause. None of the conspirators were ever charged with the crime and all three were ultimately pardoned by Eamon de Valera, head of the Irish Republic. "Big Bill" helped organize the Connolly Column of Irish volunteers who fought on the side of the Spanish Republic in the Spanish Civil War (1936–1939). The American author John Dos Passos accompanied Ernest Hemingway to Spain in 1937 to witness and report on the war. Dos Passos grew disgusted with the activities of Soviet political officers advising on the Republican side, returned to America, and later condemned the activities of the Communist Party.

"Helldivers": Naval Air Station Grosse Ile, located in the lower Detroit River, was operational from 1927 to 1969. During World War II, over five thousand American pilots, mostly Navy cadets, received training at Grosse Ile, along with over a thousand British RAF trainees. The list of airmen trained at NASGI include George H. W. Bush, forty-first president of the United States, and the actor Paul Newman.

"Ventrilo": The Ventrilo was a small device for calling birds, advertised for mail-order sale in the back pages of American comic books in the 1950s and '60s. The advertisements suggested that the device would help its user to "throw [their] voice" in the manner of a trained ventriloquist, but a careful reading of the advertisements revealed that the only aid the bird-calling device actually offered would come in the form of an accompanying pamphlet on ventriloquism. The Day of the Wren is an annual festival celebrated on December 26 (the feast day of Saint Stephen) in some sections of Ireland, particularly in the west. One story holds that the wren, the "King of All Birds," earned its title by using its distinctive song to lead a pursuing group of Norsemen away from an injured Saint Stephen. The saint escaped; the wren was eventually caught and killed by the pursuing brigands. Most commonly, the festival tradition consists of "hunting" a wren (now a "dummy" but previously a real bird) and stringing it near the top of a decorated pole. The crowds of wren boys and musicians celebrate the wren (also pronounced *wran*) by parading in masks, straw suits, and colorful outfits. At various stops along the parade route, the wren boys sing for donations to "buy the wren a grave." Any monies contributed are generally used to fund a party at a local public house after the parade. Songs about the story of the wren can be heard on *The Bells of Dublin* (1991), an album of traditional Irish music by the Chieftains.

"At Mercywood, Theodore Roethke Instructs . . .": Mercywood (1925–1986) was a residential psychiatric care facility in Ann Arbor, Michigan, operated by the Sisters of Mercy. Before he was a patient at Mercywood in the winter of 1935–1936, the poet Theodore Roethke had been teaching at Michigan State College (University) in East Lansing.

"*The Song from Moulin Rouge* (1953)": The titular song, also known as "It's April Again" and "Where Is Your Heart?," is from the 1952 film *Moulin Rouge*, directed by John Huston and starring Jose Ferrer as the French artist Toulouse-Lautrec. The most popular recording of the song in America was made in 1953 by Percy Faith and His Orchestra, with a vocal by Felicia Sanders. It reached the Billboard charts on March 28, 1953, and lasted twenty-four weeks there, finishing as the number one song for 1953.

"Nabokov at Big Da's Drive-In": The writer Vladimir Nabokov (1899–1977) was a renowned amateur lepidopterist. Among his most famous finds is the "Karner Blue" butterfly, *Lycaeides melissa samuelis* (Nabokov, 1944), which lives in only a few isolated colonies, primarily in the Great Lakes states, including Michigan. He often traveled through Michigan in his search for the Karner Blue and other species. In 1957, "Butterfly" was a number one hit for singer Andy Williams. The motion picture is *Nightfall* (1956), a film noir directed by

Jacques Tourneur and starring Aldo Ray, Brian Keith, and Anne Bancroft. Ray's character accidentally ends up with a briefcase containing $350,000 stolen in a bank robbery. By the end of the film, a snowblower mounted on the front of a semitruck consumes "Red" (Rudy Bond), the final extant bad guy, and all ends well for Ray and Bancroft.

"Slumgullion": The cartoon with Heckle and Jeckle is "The Power of Thought" (1948), directed by Eddie Donnelly.

"Slowdown": In the 1950s, the United Auto Workers, headed by Walter Reuther, began development of a vacation resort for union members on Black Lake, near Onaway, Michigan. Reuther's body is buried there.

"Letter to Dowsie, from Roethke in Ireland": See Richard Murphy's *The Kick: A Memoir of the Poet Richard Murphy* (2017), 180–187. Turlough O'Carolan (c.1670–1738) was a blind harp player and singer who is considered to be Ireland's national composer. During his career, he wandered about Ireland teaching and popularizing Celtic music. The Virtues are in the second order of angels (Dominions, Virtues, Powers) and are, in part, concerned with travel. They are said to facilitate the movement of spiritual beings to and from the physical world. The word "squadroon" is an intentional misspelling or alternate spelling of *squadron*. Cf: *The Squadroon* (1920), a memoir of World War I by Ardern Arthur Hulme Beaman.

"*Crash Injures Six Children . . .*": In 1961, the Detroit Tigers won an astonishing 101 games and still finished 8 games behind the New York Yankees in the American League pennant race. 1961 was the year that Roger Maris hit 61 home runs in 162 regular season games with the Yankees, to break Babe Ruth's single-season home run record of 60, set in 1927, during a 154-game season. A race for "pink slips" is a form of illegal street drag racing in which the loser signs over ownership (the "pink slip") of his car to the winner.

"Child atop a Half-Constructed . . .": This poem is a genuflection toward Theodore Roethke's "Child on Top of a Greenhouse," which can be found in *The Collected Poems of Theodore Roethke* (New York: Anchor Books, 1974).

"*Destination Moon*": The titular 1950 film, directed by Irving Pichel, is a dramatic full-length feature intended to show how manned spaceflight to the moon might be possible. In the famous Woody Woodpecker segment, the animated bird advises a group of scientists and investors how such a flight might best be accomplished. During World War II, Woody Woodpecker sometimes appeared as "nose art" on American warplanes, often in one of his early configurations as "crazy Woody."

"The Nazarene": There are at least four "original" versions of *Pity* (1795) by the poet and artist William Blake (1757–1827). The originals are color prints on paper, finished in ink and watercolor. Later reproductions may suggest a darker figure reaching down "to lift the child from the arms of its cataleptic mother."

"Blue Racer": See Genesis 3:15.

"The Coney Island Translations": See Acts of the Apostles 2:2–2:4 and Genesis 32:22–32:32.

"Bull Thistles": The reference is to the painting *The Lawrence Tree* by Georgia O'Keefe (1929). The tree, a ponderosa pine, still stands at the D. H. Lawrence Ranch in Taos, New Mexico. The painting itself is in the permanent collection of the Wadsworth Atheneum, Hartford, Connecticut.

"*Deus ex Machina*": The Greek philosopher Pythagoras of Samos (c. 570–495 BCE) is sometimes known as the father of mathematics. He is generally credited with the discovery of the Pythagorean theorem, which concerns right triangles. The phrase "Jack Yates blues" is a reference to the paintings of Jack B. Yeats (1871–1957). The Bible's book of Tobit is considered canonical for Roman Catholics and members of Orthodox churches, but is not in the Jewish canon, nor in most Protestants denominations, where it is considered to be part of the Apocrypha. The book of Tobit tells the story of Tobias's journey to collect a debt owed to Tobit, his blind father. Through the miraculous interventions of the angel Raphael, Tobias catches a large fish, collects the debt, defeats a demon, finds a wife, and returns home to cure his father's blindness.

Acknowledgments

I am grateful to the following institutions and publications, where versions of these poems have previously been published: *Action, Spectacle*: "Checker Cab"; *America: The Jesuit Review*: "I'm Never Told of Family Funerals"; *Atlanta Review*: "Annie Kelly, 25" and "My Grandfather's Herringbone Cap"; *Bellingham Review*: "To Tell the Hornets" (selected by Oliver de la Paz as winner of the *Bellingham Review*'s 2018 49th Parallel Prize in Poetry); *Broad River Review*: "Winter Flounder"; *Cathexis Northwest*: "Because I Wish to Avoid Extravagant Claims, and Because God Is Patient with the Unborn" and "That Fall"; *Catholic Poetry Room*: "The Adoration"; *Chestnut Review*: "Elegy with Blue-Handled Filet Knife"; *Chicago Literati*: "The Marsh Harrier" and "Last Letter from Great-Aunt Nora Gannon, Resident at St. Margaret's House of Industry (Infirmity Ward), Dublin, to Her American Nephew, Concerning the Spanish Civil War, John Dos Passos, Etc."; *Crosswinds Poetry Journal*: "Blue Racer"; *Dappled Things*: "Grievous Angel" and "*St. Brendan and the Foaming Sea* (1964)"; *2021 Fish Anthology* (Ireland): "Letter to Dowsie, from Roethke in Ireland" (selected by Billy Collins as winner of the 2021 International *Fish* Prize in Poetry); *The Flexible Persona*: "At Mercywood, Theodore Roethke Instructs My Mother in the Care and Feeding of Peonies" and "The Nazarene"; *The Grief Diaries*: "The Coney Island Translations"; *High Shelf*: "*Deus ex Machina*"; *Innisfree Poetry Journal*: "Among the 796 Dead Children at Bon Secours Mother and Baby Home, Tuam, County Galway" and "*The State of Maine*"; *Lanier Library Newsletter*: "Burning Out the Redwings," "Helldivers," and "Turnips"; *Madison Review*: "*Crash Injures Six Children; Two Serious*"; *Magnolia Review*: "Cotton House Fire"; *Midwest Review*: "Resonator"; *NARRATIVE*: "Age 10, I Escape from the Work Farm and Pursuant to Court Order, Am Recaptured in a Cincinnati Amusement Park"; *North American Review*: "Slowdown"; *Presence: A Journal of Catholic Poetry*: "The Feast of St. Blaise"; *Prometheus Dreaming*: "Dowsie Gannon, Age 2, in Cleveland" and "Ventrilo"; *Sepia Quarterly*: "In Search of a Drinkie, Mam Sneaks Out of Assisted Living to Visit *The Blue Merrow*"; *Sheila Na Gig*: "*Angela Sweets, Black Pearls, Columbia Stars*"; *Shenandoah*: "Shotgun Death, with Dodge and Northern Catalpa"; *Southeast Review*: "Nabokov at Big Da's Drive-In"; *Southword Journal* (Ireland): "Washpoosh Man" and "Jim Gannon with Dog and Model A, January 12, 1928"; *Sundog*: "Bull Thistles"; *Swannanoa Review*: "*Experts Hope to Blow Out Oil Fire on Tuesday*"; *Third Wednesday*: "Beneath the Clock Tower, Main Gate"; *Tiferet*: "Greetings"; *Tupelo Quarterly*: "Early at Big Da's Drive-In," "*Jack Kennedy Whistle-Stops across Southern Michigan*," "Shuffle Puck, 1961," "Slumgullion," and "To Recite the Mysteries"; *W. B. Yeats Society of New York*: "In a Dream, My Father Decides to Go Ice Fishing" and "Night Work" (originally published under the title "Barley Child"); *Walloon Writers Review*: "Blue Racer" (reprinted), "In a Dream, My Father Decides to Go Ice Fishing" (reprinted), "*Missing Woman Found Alive in Quarry*," "Reliquary," and "That Fall" (reprinted); *Water-Stone Review*: "*The Song from Moulin Rouge* (1953)"; and *Woodward Review*: "*Portrait of a Woman between 1948 and 1949*."

"The Marsh Harrier," "Last Letter from Great-Aunt Nora Gannon, Resident at St. Margaret's House of Industry (Infirmity Ward), Dublin, to Her American Nephew, Concerning the Spanish Civil War, John Dos Passos, Etc.," and "Ventrilo" also appeared in the limited-edition chapbook *A Short List of Breton Birds* (Sand Creek Press, 2024).

My everlasting thanks to the extraordinary poet Patricia Smith, editor of the Miller Williams Poetry Series at the University of Arkansas Press, for picking my manuscript for the 2025 Miller Williams Prize in Poetry. My thanks to the editorial staff at the University of Arkansas Press for their marvelous and unflagging work at assuring the publication of this book. My particular thanks to the marvelous and indefatigable managing editor Janet Foxman. You are a champion!

To Jack Ridl and Jane Harrington Bach—who read these poems at our monthly meetings over the course of several years—for their interest, good advice, and support. To the poet Leslie Harrison, always encouraging and brilliant; thank you. To the Irish poet and editor Patrick Cotter. To Father Michael Maher SJ, for his continuing encouragement and insightful reading of these poems. To the brilliant poet Jennifer Sperry Steinorth. My great thanks also to the poets Oliver de la Paz and Billy Collins for selecting poems among these for two wonderful publication prizes.

My special thanks to the extraordinary poets Eleanor Wilner and Maurice Manning for their generous reading and support of the *Barley Child* manuscript, and for helping me get every poem and line in (what seemed to me) their best form and place. My thanks also to the Alumni Association of the MFA Program for Writers at Warren Wilson College in Asheville, North Carolina,

and especially to the brilliant Emily Pease, to Rose Auslander, David Reukberg, Babo Kamel Edwards, Wendell Hawken Clutterbuck, Karen Llagas, and Mark Prudowsky. Thanks also to Kristina Marie Darling, Kirsten Miles, and Jeffrey Levine for critical help and encouragement through the final manuscript stages of *Barley Child*.

My thanks to Reggie Harper, to Sherry Jetter, and to the novelist Gay Hudson for their careful readings of this manuscript and their good advice. My additional thanks to the International Trudgers, who helped carry us through the COVID pandemic and beyond with grace and fellowship.

My great thanks also to Hope College, to the faculty and staff of the Hope College English Department, and to the wonderful students through the years who have supported my writing with encouragement and enthusiasm. You are the best!

My continuing debt for their lifetime bodies of work, and for the support and friendship through the years, of the writers Dan Gerber, Robert VanderMolen, Michael Delp, the late Judith Minty, the late Jim Harrison, and the recently departed Jack Driscoll. Without your help, encouragement, and legacy, I could not call myself a poet.

Finally, my greatest thank you to my wife, Marcia Kennedy Rappleye, our four children, and my brothers and sisters and their families.

Please note, the events and people depicted in these poems are, with few exceptions, entirely fictitious. No resemblance to any actual events, or to any persons, living or dead, is intended by the author. Anyone who claims to recall any of the events or to recognize any persons depicted herein is either mistaken or a survivor of things which, frankly, never occurred.